SENSORDEVICES 2024

The Fifteenth International Conference on Sensor Device Technologies and Applications

November 3rd - 7th, 2024

Nice, France

SENSORDEVICES 2024 Editors

Manuela Vieira, CTS-UNINOVA, Portugal

Arcady Zhukov, University Basque Country (UPV/EHU) and IKERBASQUE, Basque Foundation for Science, Bilbao, Spain

Printed from e-media with permission by:

Curran Associates, Inc.
57 Morehouse Lane
Red Hook, NY 12571

Some format issues inherent in the e-media version may also appear in this print version.

International Academy, Research, and Industry Association (IARIA)
412 Derby Way
Wilmington, DE 19810

Phone: (408) 893-6407
Fax: (408) 527-6351

petre@iaria.org

Additional copies of this publication are available from:

Curran Associates, Inc.
57 Morehouse Lane
Red Hook, NY 12571 USA
Phone: 845-758-0400
Fax: 845-758-2633
Email: curran@proceedings.com
Web: www.proceedings.com

Table of Contents

SENSORDEVICES 2024

Forward

The Fifteenth International Conference on Sensor Device Technologies and Applications (SENSORDEVICES 2024), held on on November 3-7, 2024, continued a series of events focusing on sensor devices themselves, the technology-capturing style of sensors, special technologies, signal control and interfaces, and particularly sensors-oriented applications. The evolution of the nano-and microtechnologies, nanomaterials, and the new business services make the sensor device industry and research on sensor-themselves very challenging.

Most of the sensor-oriented research and industry initiatives are focusing on sensor networks, data security, exchange protocols, energy optimization, and features related to intermittent connections. Recently, the concept of Internet-of-things gathers attention, especially when integrating IPv4 and IIPv6 networks. We welcomed technical papers presenting research and practical results, position papers addressing the pros and cons of specific proposals, such as those being discussed in the standard fora or in industry consortia, survey papers addressing the key problems and solutions on any of the above topics short papers on work in progress, and panel proposals.

We take here the opportunity to warmly thank all the members of the SENSORDEVICES 2024 technical program committee, as well as all the reviewers. The creation of such a high quality conference program would not have been possible without their involvement. We also kindly thank all the authors who dedicated much of their time and effort to contribute to SENSORDEVICES 2024. We truly believe that, thanks to all these efforts, the final conference program consisted of top quality contributions.

We also thank the members of the SENSORDEVICES 2024 organizing committee for their help in handling the logistics and for their work that made this professional meeting a success.

We hope that SENSORDEVICES 2024 was a successful international forum for the exchange of ideas and results between academia and industry and to promote further progress in the area of sensor devices technologies and applications. We also hope that Nice provided a pleasant environment during the conference and everyone saved some time to enjoy the historic charm of the city.

SENSORDEVICES 2024 Chairs

SENSORDEVICES 2024 Steering Committee

Arcady Zhukov, University of Basque Country (UPV/EHU), San Sebastian / Ikerbasque, Basque Foundation for Science, Bilbao, Spain
Narito Kurata, Tsukuba University of Technology, Japan
Sazzadur Chowdhury. University of Windsor, Canada
Manuela Vieira, CTS/ISEL/IPL, Portugal
Toshihiko Kiwa, Okayama University, Japan

SENSORDEVICES 2024 Publicity Chair

Lorena Parra Boronat, Universitat Politecnica de Valencia, Spain
Laura Garcia, Universidad Politécnica de Cartagena, Spain

SENSORDEVICES 2024

Committee

Fulvio Re Cecconi, Politecnico di Milano, Italy
Tao Chen, University of Pittsburgh, USA
Irinela Chilibon, National Institute of Research and Development for Optoelectronics - INOE-2000, Romania
Raad Farhood Chisab, Middle Technical University, Baghdad, Iraq
Nan-Fu Chiu, National Taiwan Normal University, Taiwan
Chi-Wai Chow, National Chiao Tung University, Hsinchu, Taiwan
Sazzadur Chowdhury, University of Windsor, Canada
Jesse R. Codling, University of Michigan - Ann Arbor, USA
Juan M. Corchado, University of Salamanca, Spain
Marco Crescentini, University of Bologna, Italy
Udhaya Kumar Dayalan, Trane Technologies, USA
Francesco G. Della Corte, Università degli Studi di Napoli Federico II, Italy
Emiliano Descrovi, Norwegian University of Science and Technology (NTNU), Trondheim, Norway / Polytechnic University of Turin, Torino, Italy
Abdou Karim Diallo,Gaston Berger University, Senegal
Dermot Diamond, Dublin City University, Ireland
Amad Ud Din, Fatima Jinnah Women University, Pakistan
Toan Dinh, University of Southern Queensland, Australia
Bahram Djafari Rouhani, University of Lille, France
René Domínguez-Cruz, Universidad Autónoma de Tamaulipas, Mexico
Mingzheng Duan, University of California Berkeley, USA
Jimmy T. Efird, CSPEC/DVAHCS/HSR&D (Duke University Affiliated Center), Durham, USA
Abdelali Elmoufidi, Hassan II University of Casablanca, Morocco
Eugenia Fagadar-Cosma, Institute of Chemistry "Coriolan Dragulescu", Timisoara, Romania
Francisco Falcone, UPNA-ISC, Spain
Vittorio Ferrari, University of Brescia, Italy
Laurent Fesquet, Grenoble Institute of Technology, France
Rui Fonseca-Pinto, Polytechnic of Leiria, Portugal
Nazila Fough, Robert Gordon University, UK
Óscar Fresnedo Arias, University of A Coruña, Spain
Mounir Gaidi, University of Sharjah, UAE
Cécile Ghouila-Houri, Centrale Lille, France
Francesca Giannone, Niccolò Cusano University, Rome, Italy
Michele Giordano, IPCB - CNR, Italy
Jan Havlík, Czech Technical University in Prague, Czech Republic
Lukas Heindler, Johannes Kepler University Linz, Austria
Johan Holmgren, Malmö University, Sweden
M. Carmen Horrillo Güemes, Group of Technology of Advanced Sensors (SENSAVAN)-ITEFI-CSIC, Spain
Wen-Jyi Hwang, National Taiwan Normal University, Taipei, Taiwan
Mohamed Ichchou, Ecole Centrale de Lyon, France
Raul Igual, EUP Teruel | University of Zaragoza, Spain
Illyas Md Isa, Universiti Pendidikan Sultan Idris, Malaysia
Kh Tohidul Islam, The University of Melbourne | Melbourne Medical School, Australia
Chi-Shih Jao, University of California, Irvine, USA
Mark Kagarura, Paderborn University, Germany / Makerere University, Uganda
Grigoris Kaltsas, University of West Attica, Greece
Rajesh Khanna, Thapar Institute of Engineering and Technology, India

Copyright Information

Spatially Distributed Annealing as a New Tuning of Magnetic Microwires

Alexander Chizhik
Department Advanced Polymers and Materials: Physics, Chemistry and Technology
University of Basque Country, UPV/EHU
San Sebastian, Spain
oleksandr.chyzhyk@ehu.eus

Arcady Zhukov
Department Advanced Polymers and Materials: Physics, Chemistry and Technology
University of Basque Country, UPV/EHU
IKERBASQUE, Basque Foundation for Science
San Sebastian, Spain
arkadi.joukov@ehu.eus

Abstract—**Spatially distributed annealing shows a new way of microwires tuning for sensors application. In this paper, we are dealing with a new, original annealing treatment. Our solution is related to the fact that, after the annealing, the distribution of magnetic properties is preserved. A gradient of internal stresses, ranging from tension to compression, was present across the sample's cross section, with the stress gradient smoothly varying along its length. Magnetic and magneto-optical studies revealed a transformation in both the magnetization reversal process and the domain structure as the measurement location shifted along the sample.**

Keywords- soft magnetic materials; amorphous magnetic microwires; magnetic domains; magneto-optic Kerr effect; magnetic anisotropy.

I. INTRODUCTION

Regarding the motivation of the presented research, there were recent studies on stress annealing on magnetic structure and Giant Magneto-Impedance effect (GMI) as well as Matteucci effects in bent microwires [1].

Our research can be considered within the framework of the idea of studying magnetic properties distributed along the length of a long sample. In addition to the distribution that was caused by annealing at temperatures distributed along the length of the microwire [2], we are now expanding this direction by adding external influences, such as distributed bending stress, along the length of the microwire, including the spiral bending. The main feature of this type of research is the smooth transition of magnetic properties along the sample, which provides great opportunities for analyzing the physical processes occurring in the sample. The original idea implemented in the presented study is that, after bending annealing and subsequent straightening of the sample, the induced magnetic properties are retained in the microwire.

II. EXPERIMENTAL TECHNIQUES

After the manufacture, the samples were bent and annealed in the bent state (T_{ann} = 300 °C (45 min)) (Figure 1). The hysteresis loops were obtained using the fluxmetric method, previously used for characterization of magnetically soft microwires. A thin (about 8 mm in diameter) 12 cm long solenoid creates a rather uniform axial

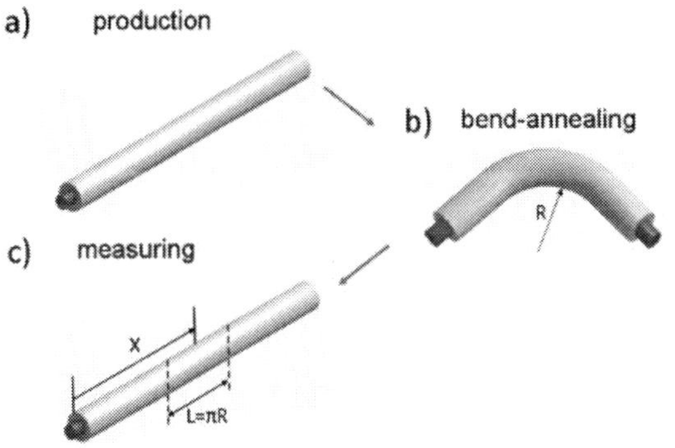

Figure 1. Schematic picture of the samples preparation for the measuring

magnetic field in the region where a sample of 10 cm long is inserted. The fluxmetric method allows the measurement of hysteresis loops up to H=3 kA/m. A short (2 mm long) pick-up coil was used to characterize the bending-annealed microwires, which can show hysteresis loops with different shapes for different regions of the microwire. Such setup allowed us to measure the hysteresis loops in different longitudinal regions of the microwire by moving the short pick-up coil along it.

The Magneto-Optical Kerr Effect (MOKE) technique has been applied as a method to acquire the contrast images of the surface magnetic domain structures. The experiments were performed by means of a high-resolution, wide-field, optical polarizing microscope based on a commercial one (Carl Zeiss) working in reflective mode using the longitudinal MOKE configuration. Also, the MOKE technique has been applied as a method to retrieve the information about the magnetization reversal (surface hysteresis loops).

III. RESULTS AND DISCUSSION

The effect of bending annealing-induced magnetic bistability was discovered in Fe rich microwires [3]. Without annealing and after the annealing without bending, this effect was not observed. The induced bistability effect was accompanied by the rapid movement of a single longitudinal domain wall along the surface of the microwire that was not observed in the classical bistability effect. The existence of the longitudinal magnetic domain structure is the result of a particular distribution of internal stress. This distribution represents a gradual transition from compression to tension across the microwire diameter.

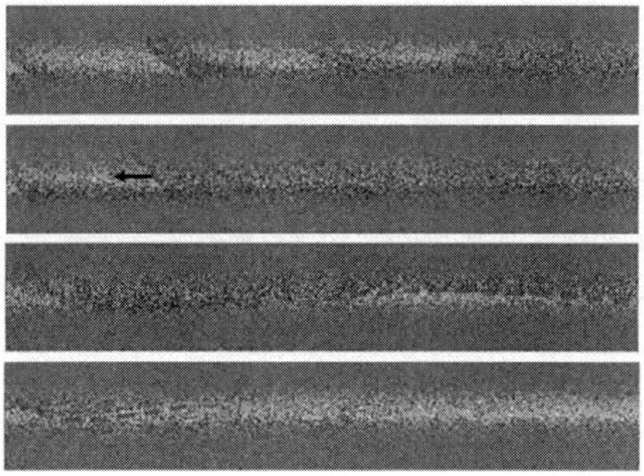

Figure 2. Samples of MOKE images of surface domain structure observed in different locations.

The external mechanical bending stress also results in an internal stress distribution within the Co-rich microwire: from maximum tensile stress at the upper side to maximum compressive stress at the bottom side [4]. Consequently, a specific line within the sample corresponds to a zero value of internal stress where tension transitions to compression. This stress distribution across the sample diameter would consequently lead to the formation of a corresponding magnetic domain structure (Figure 2).

IV. CONCLUSION

The presented investigations were devoted to the studying of the magnetic properties of Co-rich microwires subjected to the so-called spiral annealing. Before annealing, the sample was laid in the form of a flat spiral. The curvature value at each point of the sample was known. The main idea was that, after annealing, we had a sample with magnetic properties continuously distributed along the length of the sample. As expected, we found a smooth change in the magnetic properties as the measurement point shifted along the sample. Changes were observed both in the sample volume and on the surface. Particular attention was paid to the induced change in the anisotropy field. A direct dependence of this effect on the value of the changing curvature of the sample was found.

Future research in this area involves expanding the pre-treatment methods, including a type of annealing called spiral annealing, which allows for mechanical stresses to be created not only along but also across the microwire. This will allow advances in optimizing the parameters of magnetic sensors.

ACKNOWLEDGMENT

Funding provided by the EU under the "INFINITE" (HORIZONCL5-2021-D5-01-06) and "Harmony" (HORIZON-CL4-2023-RESILIENCE-01) projects, by the Spanish MICIN under the PID2022-141373NB-I00 project, by Elkartek (MINERVA, MAGAF, and MOSINCO) projects, and under the scheme of "Ayuda a Grupos Consolidados" (ref. IT1670-22). The authors are grateful for the technical and human support provided by SGIker of UPV/EHU (Medidas Magneticas Gipuzkoa) and European funding (ERDF and ESF).

REFERENCES

[1] J. Nabias, A. Asfour and J. P. Yonnet, "The Impact of bending stress on the performance of Giant Magneto-Impedance (GMI) magnetic sensors", *Sensors*, vol. 17, p. 640, 2017.

[2] A. Chizhik, P. Corte-Leon, V. Zhukova, J. Gonzalez, P. Gawronski, J. M. Blanco and A. Zhukov, "Determination of Magnetic Structures in Magnetic Microwires with Longitudinally Distributed Magnetic Anisotropy" *Sensors*, vol. 23, p. 3079, 2023.

[3] A. Chizhik, P. Corte-Leon, V. Zhukova and A. Zhukov, "Bend induced magnetic bistability in amorphous microwires", *Materials Technology*, vol. 38, article 2282318, 2023.

[4] A. Chizhik, P. Corte-Leon, V. Zhukova and A. Zhukov, "Bending annealing induced transformation of magnetic structure in Co-rich amorphous microwires", *Physica B*, vol. 689, article 416178, 2024.

Magnetic Properties and GMI Effect in Multilayered Co-rich Microwires

Valentina Zhukova, Alvaro Gonzalez
Department of Polymers and Advance Materials,
Univ. Basque Country, UPV/EHU, 20018
San Sebastian, Spain
e-mail: valentina.zhukova@ehu.es, alvaro.gonzalezv@ehu.eus

Ricardo López Antón, Juan Pedro Gonzalez, Juan Antonio González
Instituto Regional de Investigación Científica Aplicada (IRICA) and Department of Applied Physics,
University of Castilla-La Mancha, 13071
Ciudad Real, Spain
e-mail: ricardo.lopez@uclm.es, juanpedro.andres@uclm.es, j.a.gonzalez@uclm.es

Arcady Zhukov
Department of Polymers and Advance Materials,
Univ. Basque Country, UPV/EHU, 20018,
San Sebastian and Ikerbasque, Bilbao Spain
e-mail: arkadi.joukov@ehu.es

Abstract—**The influence of magnetic and non-magnetic layers deposited by magnetic sputtering onto glass-coated amorphous Co-rich microwires on magnetic properties and Giant Magnetoimpedance (GMI) effect has been analyzed. The magnetic and non-magnetic layers affect both the hysteresis loop and the magnetic field dependence of the GMI ratio. The contributions from the internal stresses originated by the sputtered layer as well as the magnetostatic interaction between the amorphous ferromagnetic nucleus and deposited magnetic layers are discussed.**

Keywords- magnetic microwires; magnetic softness; hysteresis loops; internal stresses; magnetic anisotropy.

I. INTRODUCTION

Amorphous materials can present excellent soft magnetic properties together with superior mechanical properties and, hence, are suitable for various applications including magnetic sensors or non-destructive wireless monitoring of composites [1]-[5].

The most unusual properties of amorphous wire are magnetic bistability associated with remagnetization process running through single and large Barkhausen jump [6]-[8] or giant magnetoimpedance, GMI, effect [9]-[12]. The GMI effect has attracted attention due to the extremely high impedance sensitivity to an external magnetic field (up to 10%/A/m) observed in magnetic microwires [12] [13]. Therefore, several high-performance magnetic sensors and magnetometers have been developed [9] [14].

The above-mentioned GMI effect consists of a noticeable change in the impedance Z of the magnetic material under the influence of an external magnetic field, H [9]-[11].

The GMI effect typically represented through the GMI ratio, $\Delta Z/Z$, defined as [9]-[11]:

$$\Delta Z/Z=[Z(H)-Z(H_{max})]/Z(H_{max})\cdot 100 \qquad (1)$$

being H_{max} the maximum applied DC magnetic field (typically a few kA/m).

The $\Delta Z/Z$ –values are substantially affected by several parameters, such as H-value as well as frequency, f, of AC current, AC current amplitude, H_{max} –value, applied and internal stress, magnetic anisotropy of studied material, etc. [9]-[11]. Therefore, for optimization of $\Delta Z/Z$ –values and achievement of maximum $\Delta Z/Z$ –values, $\Delta Z/Z_m$, several parameters must be considered. Thus, at fixed f,-value the $\Delta Z/Z(H)$ dependence can have the maximum either at H=0 or can present symmetric double-peak dependence with two maxima at H-value attributed to transverse magnetic anisotropy field. Meanwhile, the optimum frequency, f_o, is related to the diameter of magnetic wire: for 120 μm diameter amorphous wires, a f_o of the order of 1 MHz is reported [12], whereas for magnetic microwires with diameters of about 15-20 μm, f_o of the order of 100 MHz is reported [11]. Accordingly, a decrease in diameter is associated with an increase in the optimal frequency range of the GMI effect [15]. Consequently, for each magnetic wire with given geometrical parameters and magnetic anisotropy type (wire diameter and chemical composition), there are optimal conditions at which the highest GMI ratio, $\Delta Z/Z_m$, is observed [11].

In amorphous magnetic wires, the best magnetic softness and, hence, the highest $\Delta Z/Z$ –values ($\Delta Z/Z_m$ about 200-300%) are typically observed in Co-rich compositions with vanishing magnetostriction coefficients, λ_s [11]. The $\Delta Z/Z_m$ –values can be further improved by appropriate post-processing. In properly post-processed magnetic microwires, $\Delta Z/Z_m$ –values of the order 600- 700% have been reported [12] [13] [17].

Recently, a new approach allowing tailoring the magnetic anisotropy of magnetic wires by depositing magnetic and non-magnetic layers onto the glass-coating was reported [18] [19].

Evidently, the performance of sensors and devices based on the GMI effect can be significantly improved by using materials with a higher GMI effect. Therefore, tuning of the

GMI effect through the modification of the magnetic anisotropy of the magnetic materials attracted substantial attention is presently [19]-[21].

Accordingly, we shall provide our latest results on tailoring of the GMI effect and magnetic properties of amorphous glass-coated microwires by magnetic (Permalloy) and non-magnetic (Cu) layers deposited by magnetic sputtering onto glass-coating.

In the section Experimental details, we present the description of the experimental techniques, while in the Experimental results and discussion section we describe the results on effect of magnetic (Permalloy) and non-magnetic (Cu) layers deposited by magnetic sputtering onto glass-coating on hysteresis loops and GMI effect of the microwires.

II. EXPERIMENTAL DETAILS

We prepared and studied hysteresis loops and GMI effect of coated microwire with magnetic (Permalloy) or non-magnetic (Cu) layers up to 600 nm thick deposited on a glass coating. Studied amorphous $Co_{67}Fe_{3.85}Ni_{1.45}B_{11.5}Si_{14.5}Mo_{1.7}$ glass-coated microwire prepared by Taylor-Ulitovsky technique, described earlier elsewhere [15].

The axial hysteresis loops were measured using the fluxmetric method [21], as well as using the Physical Property Magnetic System (PPMS) vibrating-sample magnetometer. For a better comparison of the studied samples, the hysteresis loops were presented as the normalized magnetization M/M_o versus H dependencies (being M - the magnetic moment at given H and M_o - the magnetic moment at the maximum employed magnetic field amplitude).

The $\Delta Z/Z\ (H)$ dependencies were evaluated using (1) from the experimentally measured $Z(H)$ dependence. Z-values were obtained from the reflection coefficient S_{11} measured using a specially designed microstrip sample holder and a vector network analyzer, as described earlier [22].

The magnetostriction coefficient, λ_s, of studied microwire was measured using the so-called Small Angle Magnetization Rotation (SAMR) method [23], recently successfully adapted for glass-coated microwires of reduced diameter [23]. The low and negative λ_s–value ($-3\cdot10^{-6}$) was obtained for studied microwire.

Thin Permalloy (Py) and copper (Cu) layers were deposited by Radio Frequency magnetron sputtering onto the glass coating of both microwires. The sample holder geometry and the deposition system allowed the continuous rotation of the sample holder (at 14 r.p.m.). Accordingly, a homogenous deposition on the surface of the glass-coating of microwire (excepting the fixed extremes) was achieved. The thickness of the thin films was 600 nm.

Hysteresis loops of single microwires have been measured using the fluxmetric method previously described in detail elsewhere [32]. In order to compare the samples with different compositions and subjected to different post-processing, we represent the hysteresis loops as the normalized magnetization, M/M_0, versus magnetic field, H, where M is the magnetic moment at a given magnetic field and M_0 is the magnetic moment of the sample at the maximum magnetic field amplitude, H_m.

III. EXPERIMENTAL RESULTS AND DISCUSSION

The hysteresis loops of studied sample prior depositing of magnetic (Permalloy) or non-magnetic (Cu) layers is typical for amorphous microwire with low negative λ_s – values. The coercivity, H_c, is about 40 A/m, as evidenced from the hysteresis loops (see Figure 1).

The contribution of magnetic layers on hysteresis loops of studied sample is shown in Figures 2 (a,b) and 3. After deposition of the layers, the low-field hysteresis loops generally tend to be more rectangular (see Figures 2 a,b). The presence of non-magnetic (Cu) layers is reflected by a

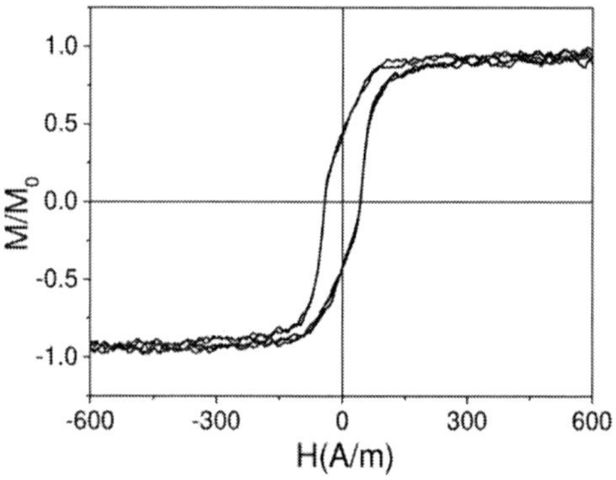

Figure 1. Hysteresis loop of as-prepared sample.

more rectangular hysteresis loop (see Figure 1). On the other hand, the presence of hysteresis observed up to rather high magnetic field must be attributed to the contribution of magnetic layer (see Figure 3).

$\Delta Z/Z(H)$ dependencies of as-prepared sample and after depositing of magnetic or non-magnetic layers are shown in Figure 4. As expected from the influence of deposited layers on hysteresis loops, the GMI ratio, $\Delta Z/Z$ and $\Delta Z/Z(H)$ dependencies are affected by the deposited layers (see Figure 4). In particular, the GMI ratio becomes generally lower after depositing any magnetic or non-magnetic layers. However, the highest GMI ratio and sharper peaks on $\Delta Z/Z(H)$ dependencies are observed in the sample with Permalloy layer.

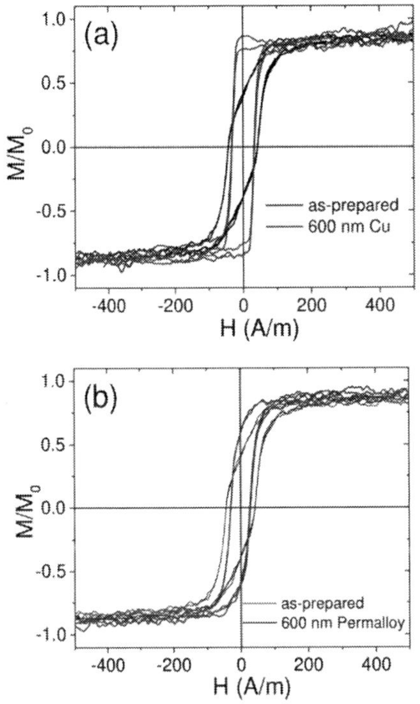

Figure 2. Low field hysteresis loop with deposited 600 nm thick non-magnetic Cu (a) and Permalloy (b) layers.

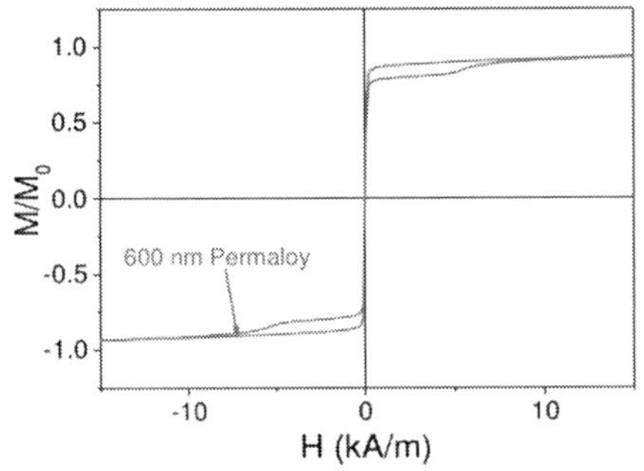

Figure 3. Hysteresis loops of magnetic microwires with Co- and Permalloy layers of the same thickness measured up to 20 kA/m.

All the *ΔZ/Z(H)* dependencies have double-peak character with maximum GMI ratio values, $\Delta Z/Z_m$, at H≠0 (see Figure 4). The evolution of *ΔZ/Z(H)* dependencies with frequency are rather different. Thus, in as-prepared sample the highest $\Delta Z/Z_m$ is observed at f=100 MHz, whereas in the samples with Cu-layer the highest $\Delta Z/Z_m$ –value is observed at f =80 MHz.

The evolution of $\Delta Z/Z_m$(f) dependencies provided in Figure 5 allows to compare the influence of the magnetic or non-magnetic deposited layers on $\Delta Z/Z_m$ –value and select optimal conditions for each sample.

For as-prepared sample and sample with Permalloy layer, the optimal frequency is about 100 MHz, where

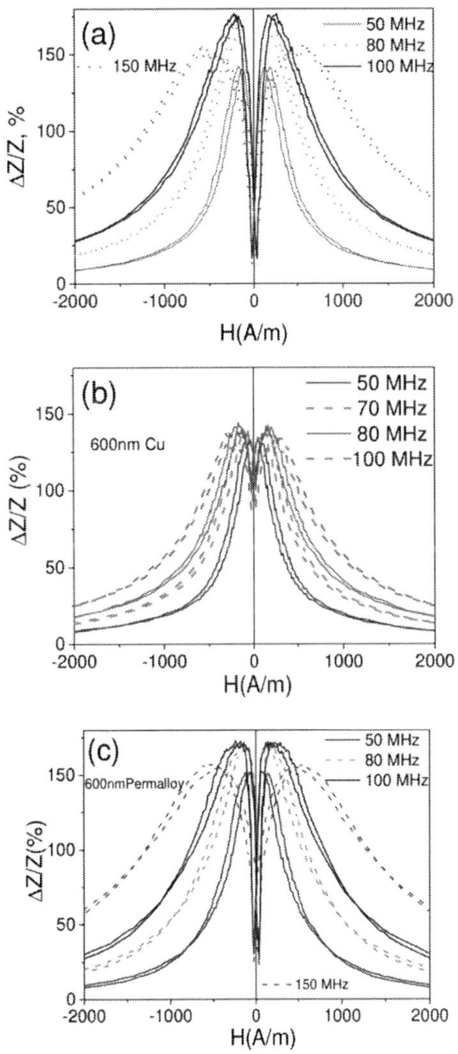

Figure 4. *ΔZ/Z(H)* dependencies of as-prepared $Co_{67}Fe_{3.85}Ni_{1.45}B_{11.5}Si_{14.5}Mo_{1.7}$ microwires (a) and of the same sample with deposited 600 nm thick layers of Cu (b) and Permalloy (c).

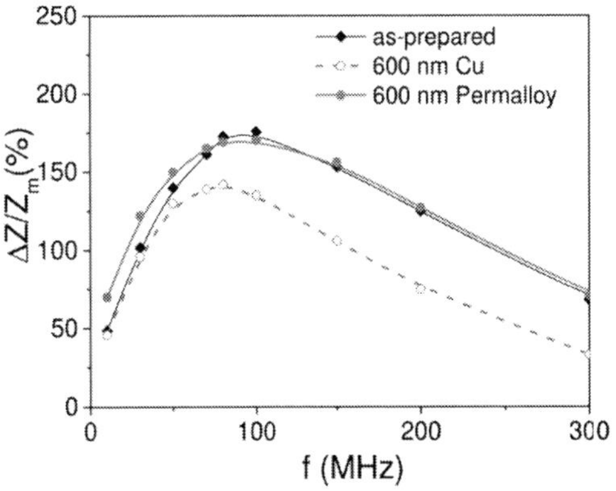

Figure 5. *ΔZ/Z$_m$(f)* dependencies of as-prepared microwire and after depositing of magnetic and non-magnetic layers.

$\Delta Z/Z_m$ ≈175% are observed. Meanwhile, for the samples with Cu layer, the optimal frequency is about 80 at which $\Delta Z/Z_m$ ≈145% are observed. In the frequency band $f \leq 100$ MHz, the sample with a permalloy layer has the highest $\Delta Z/Z_m$ –values.

For interpretation of the obtained experimental results, we must consider two types of effects. Thus, both magnetic and non-magnetic layers deposited on the glass-coating affect the internal stresses distribution inside the metallic nucleus arising during the glass-coated microwires preparation. As previously shown [19][25], the presence of the metallic layers deposited on the glass-coating results in the onset of the additional compressive stresses. The compressive nature of the stresses induced by the deposited metallic layers is confirmed by the modification of the hysteresis loops (see Figure 2): after the deposition of metallic layers, all low-field hysteresis loops become more rectangular.

On the other hand, the different character of the hysteresis loops, $\Delta Z/Z_m$ –values and $\Delta Z/Z(H)$ dependencies in the samples with non-magnetic (Cu) and magnetic (Permalloy) must be related to the magnetic properties of the layer deposited on the glass-coating. Thus, a magnetic layer in its remanence state can produce a stray field that should affect both hysteresis loops and GMI behavior of amorphous magnetically soft nucleus. The existence of the magnetostatic interaction between two magnetic microwires with different magnetic properties has been recently experimentally observed in array consisting of magnetically soft Co-rich microwire and magnetically harder Fe-rich microwire [26].

IV. CONCLUSIONS AND FUTURE WORK

We showed that the magnetic properties and GMI effect of amorphous magnetic microwires can be tuned by magnetic and non-magnetic layers deposited onto glass-coating. In studying Co-rich microwires with deposited magnetic and non-magnetic layers, we observed substantial effect of deposited magnetic and non-magnetic layers on GMI effect and hysteresis loops. Low field hysteresis loops of studied microwire present systematic change upon deposition of non-magnetic and magnetic layers towards more rectangular hysteresis loops. The GMI ratio and its magnetic field dependencies are affected by the presence of magnetic and non-magnetic layers deposited onto glass-coating. The observed experimental dependencies are discussed considering both change of the internal stresses originated by the deposited layers as well as the magnetostatic interaction between the amorphous ferromagnetic nucleus and deposited magnetic layer. In the future, the influence of magnetically harder layers deposited onto the glass-coating and effect of the deposited magnetic layer thickness on hysteresis loops and GMI effect will be studied. It is expected to tune the magnetostatic interaction between the amorphous ferromagnetic nucleus and deposited magnetic layer and thus modify the magnetic field dependence of the GMI ratio.

ACKNOWLEDGMENT

This work was supported by EU under "INFINITE" (HORIZON-CL5-2021-D5-01-06) and "Harmony" (HORIZON-CL4-2023-RESILIENCE-01) projects, by the Spanish MICIN, under PID2022-141373NB-I00 project, by the Government of the Basque Country under PUE_2021_1_0009, Elkartek (MOSINCO and ATLANTIS) projects and under the scheme of "Ayuda a Grupos Consolidados" (ref. IT1670-22), and by the "Plan Propio de la Universidad de Castilla-La Mancha" (FEDER, EU) 2022-GRIN-34313. The authors are thankful for the technical and human support provided by SGIker of UPV/EHU (Medidas Magneticas Gipuzkoa) and European funding (ERDF and ESF).

REFERENCES

[1] J. Durand, "Magnetic Properties of Metallic Glasses" in Topics in Applied Physics, vol. 53, 1983, Glassy Metals II. Atomic and Dynamics, Electronic Structure, Magnetic Properties, Editors: H. Beck and H. -J. Güntherodt, Springer-Verlag, Berlin, Heidelberg, New York, Tokyo.

[2] A. P. Zhukov, "The remagnetization process of bistable amorphous alloys", Mater. Des., vol. 5, pp. 299-305, 1993.

[3] M. Hagiwara, A. Inoue, and T. Masumoto, "Mechanical properties of Fe–Si–B amorphous wires produced by in-rotating-water spinning method", Metall. Trans. A., vol. 13, pp. 373-382, 1982.

[4] T. Goto, M. Nagano, and N. Wehara, "Mechanical properties of amorphous $Fe_{80}P_{16}C_3B_1$ filament produced by glass-coated melt spinning", Trans. JIM, vol. 18, pp. 759-764, 1997.

[5] D. C. Jiles, "Recent advances and future directions in magnetic materials", Acta Mater., vol. 51, pp. 5907-5939, 2003.

[6] K. Mohri, F.B. Humphrey, K. Kawashima, K. Kimura and M. Muzutani, "Large Barkhausen and Matteucci effects in FeCoSiB, FeCrSiB, and FeNiSiB amorphous wires", IEEE Trans. Magn., vol. 26, pp. 1789-1781, 1990.

[7] M. Vázquez and D.-X. Chen, "The magnetization reversal process in amorphous wires", IEEE Trans. Magn., vol. 31, no. 2, pp. 1229-1239, 1995.

[8] A. Zhukov et al., "Advanced functional magnetic microwires for technological applications", J. Phys. D: Appl. Phys. vol. 55, p. 253003, 2022.

[9] K. Mohri, T. Uchiyama, L. P. Shen, C. M. Cai and L. V. Panina, "Amorphous wire and CMOS IC-based sensitive micro-magnetic sensors (MI sensor and SI sensor) for intelligent measurements and controls", J. Magn. Magn. Mater., vol. 249, pp. 351-356, 2001.

[10] M. Knobel, M. Vazquez and L. Kraus, "Giant magnetoimpedance", Handbook Magn. Mater., vol. 15, pp. 497- 563, 2003.

[11] A. Zhukov et al., "Giant magnetoimpedance in rapidly quenched materials," J. Alloy Compd., vol. 814, p. 152225, 2020.

[12] K. R. Pirota, L. Kraus, H. Chiriac and M. Knobel, "Magnetic properties and GMI in a CoFeSiB glass-covered microwire", J. Magn. Magn. Mater., vol. 21, p. L243-L247, 2000.

[13] A. Zhukov, V. Zhukova, J. M. Blanco and J. Gonzalez "Recent research on magnetic properties of glass-coated microwires", J. Magn. Magn., Mater. vol. 294, pp. 182-192, 2005.

[14] Y. Honkura and S. Honkura, "The Development of ASIC Type GSR Sensor Driven by GHz Pulse Current", Sensors, vol. 20, p. 1023, 2020.

[15] P. Aragoneses, A. Zhukov, J. Gonzalez, J. M. Blanco and L. Dominguez, "Effect of AC driving current on Magneto-Impedance effect", Sens. Actuators A, vol. 81/1-3, pp. 86-90, 2000.

[16] D. Ménard, M. Britel, P. Ciureanu and A. Yelon, "Giant magneto-impedance in a cylindrical conductor", J. Appl. Phys., vol. 84 (5), pp. 2805–2814, 1998.
[17] P. Corte-León et al., "Engineering of magnetic properties of Co-rich microwires by joule heating", Intermetallics, vol. 105, pp. 92-98, 2019.
[18] K.R. Pirota, M. Hernandez-Velez, D. Navas, A. Zhukov and M. Vázquez, "Multilayer microwires: tailoring magnetic behavior by sputtering and electroplating", Adv. Funct. Mater., vol. 14 No 3, pp. 266-268, 2004.
[19] J. Torrejón, G. Badini, K. Pirota and M. Vázquez, "Design of multilayer microwires with controllable magnetic properties: Magnetostatic and magnetoelastic coupling", Acta materialia vol. 55, pp. 4271-4276, 2007
[20] J. Torrejón, M. Vázquez and L. V. Panina, "Asymmetric magnetoimpedance in self-biased layered CoFe/CoNi microwires", J. Appl. Phys. vol. 105, p. 033911, 2009.
[21] L. Gonzalez-Legarreta et al., "Optimization of magnetic properties and GMI effect of Thin Co-rich Microwires for GMI Microsensors", Sensors, vol. 20, p. 1558, 2020.
[22] A. Zhukov et al., "Routes for Optimization of Giant Magnetoimpedance Effect in Magnetic Microwires", IEEE Instrum. Meas. Mag. vol. 23(1), pp. 56-63, 2020.
[23] K. Narita, J. Yamasaki and H. Fukunaga, "Measurement of saturation magnetostriction of a thin Amorphous Ribbon by Means of Small-Angle Magnetization Rotation", IEEE Trans. Magn. Vol. Mag-16, pp. 435-439, 1980.
[24] M. Churyukanova et al., "Magnetostriction investigation of soft magnetic microwires", Phys. Stat. Sol. A., vol. 213(2), pp. 363–367, 2016.
[25] M. Vazquez, K. Pirota, J. Torrejon, G. Badini and A. Torcunov, "Magnetoelastic interactions in multilayer microwires", J. Magn. Magn. Mater. vol. 304, pp. 197–202, 2006.
[26] P. Corte-Leon et al., "Controlling of the single domain wall propagation in magnetic microwires by magnetostatic interaction", J. Sci.: Adv. Mater. Devices, vol. 9, p. 100712, 2024.

Optimization of GMI Effect and Magnetic Softness of Co-rich Microwires

Paula Corte-Leon, Valentina Zhukova, Alvaro Gonzalez
Department of Polymers and Advance Materials, Univ. Basque Country, UPV/EHU, 20018 San Sebastian, Spain
e-mail: paula.corte@ehu.eus; valentina.zhukova@ehu.es, alvaro.gonzalezv@ehu.eus

Juan Maria Blanco
Dept. Appl. Phys. I, EIG, Univ. Basque Country, UPV/EHU, 20018, San Sebastian, Spain
e-mail: juanmaria.blanco@ehu.eus

Arcady Zhukov
Dept Polymers and Advance Materials Physics, Univ. Basque Country, UPV/EHU, 20018 San Sebastian and Ikerbasque, Bilbao Spain
e-mail: arkadi.joukov@ehu.es

Abstract—**We provide our attempts to improve the Giant Magneto-Impedance (GMI) effect and magnetic softness of Co-rich glass-coated magnetic microwires by annealing. We studied the effect of annealing on the hysteresis loops and the GMI ratio of Co-rich microwires. A remarkable GMI ratio improvement up to 735% is observed after annealing of Co-rich microwires under appropriate conditions. The observed magnetic softening and GMI ratio improvement are discussed considering the internal stresses relaxation and a change in the magnetostriction coefficient sign and values after annealing.**

Keywords- magnetic microwires; magnetic softness; GMI effect; internal stresses; magnetic anisotropy.

I. INTRODUCTION

The main interest in amorphous magnetic materials is an excellent magnetic softness combined with superior mechanical and corrosion properties [1][2]. The most common method for preparation of amorphous materials is rapid quenching from the melt [1]-[3]. Such technique allows preparation of either amorphous ribbons or wires [3] [4].

The main interest in amorphous wires is related to the highest Giant Magneto-Impedance, GMI, effect [4]-[6] commonly attributed to high circumferential magnetic permeability, μ_ϕ, of amorphous wires and substantial μ_ϕ dependence on the applied magnetic field.

The most common way to represent the GMI effect is the GMI ratio, $\Delta Z/Z$, given as [4]-[6]:

$$\Delta Z/Z=[Z(H)-Z(H_{max})]/Z(H_{max})\cdot 100 \quad (1)$$

where Z is the sample impedance, H is the applied magnetic field and H_{max} is the maximum applied Direct Current, DC, magnetic field (usually below a few Oe).

Typically, $\Delta Z/Z$ –values of about 200-300% are reported in Co-rich magnetic wires with vanishing magnetostriction coefficients, λ_s [4]-[6]. In several publications, $\Delta Z/Z$ –values above 600% have been achieved in carefully processed Co-rich wires [6]-[8].

There are several fabrication processes involving rapid melt quenching allowing preparation of amorphous magnetic wires. Recently the main attention is paid to studies of glass-coated microwires. The main reasons are the most extended range of metallic nucleus diameters (from 0.1 to 100 μm), as well as better corrosion properties and biocompatibility related to the presence of flexible and insulating glass-coating [9]-[12]. Such glass-coated microwires can be prepared using the so-called modified Taylor-Ulitovsky (also known as quenching-and-drawing method), actually known since the 60s and intensively studied since the 90s [9]-[14].

The performance of sensors and devices based on use of the GMI effect is substantially affected by the $\Delta Z/Z$ - value. Therefore, great attention was paid to studies of the magnetic wires with improved magnetic softness and optimization of the GMI effect by thermal treatment [7][8].

Consequently, in this paper we provide our latest attempt on optimization of the magnetic softness and GMI effect in Co-rich glass-coated magnetic microwires.

In Section 2, we present the description of the experimental methods and samples, while in Section 3, we describe the results on effect of annealing on hysteresis loops and GMI effect of Co-rich microwires. We conclude our work in Section 4.

II. EXPERIMENTAL DETAILS

We prepared Co-rich $Co_{72}Fe_4B_{13}Si_{11}$ glass-coated amorphous microwires with metallic nucleus diameter, d, of about 40 μm and a total diameter, D, of about 45 μm by the aforementioned Taylor-Ulitovsky method [9]-[12]. The chemical composition was selected considering nearly-zero magnetostriction coefficient, λ_s ($\lambda_s \approx 10^{-7}$) of Co-rich Co-Fe based amorphous alloys [15] [16].

Axial hysteresis loops were measured using the fluxmetric method, developed for studies of soft magnetic microwires with reduced diameters [17]. All the measurements were performed at room temperature. The electromotive force, ϵ, in the pick-up coil with N turns produced by the change of magnetic flux, ϕ, is given by [17]:

$$\epsilon = -N\frac{d\phi}{dt} \quad (2)$$

The change in magnetic flux originates by the sample magnetization, M, and by the applied magnetic field, H. The compensation coil was used to eliminate the magnetic flux component originated by the applied magnetic field. This compensation coil is connected in series- opposition with the pick-up coil. In numerous previous studies this experimental setup was successfully used for measurements of the hysteresis loops of extremely soft magnetic microwires allowing mA/m resolution of coercivity [6][8][17]. The hysteresis loops represented as the normalized magnetization M/M_o versus applied magnetic field, H (being M_o -the magnetic moment of the samples at maximum amplitude H_o of magnetic field) allows better comparison of magnetic properties of studied microwires with different chemical compositions and diameters. The GMI ratio, $\Delta Z/Z$, was defined using (1) from the $Z(H)$ dependence. Z-values were evaluated using a vector network analyzer from the reflection coefficient S_{11}, as described elsewhere [17].

The amorphous state studied sample has been confirmed by a broad halo in the X-ray spectra obtained using X-ray diffraction.

A recently developed setup designed to evaluate the λ_s of magnetic microwires using the so-called Small Angle Magnetization Rotation (SAMR) method was used for λ_s measurements [19].

We studied as-prepared microwires and microwires annealed in conventional furnace at 300 °C.

III. EXPERIMENTAL RESULTS AND DISCUSSION

As can be seen from the hysteresis loop (see Figure 1), as-prepared microwires present rather soft magnetic properties with coercivities, H_c, about 20 A/m and magnetic anisotropy fields, H_k, below 200 A/m.

This behavior is typical for amorphous microwire with low negative λ_s –values.

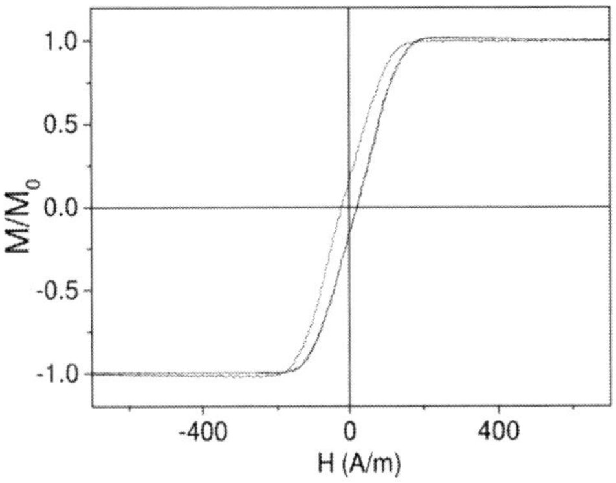

Figure 1. Hysteresis loops of $Co_{72}Fe_4B_{13}Si_{11}$ microwires with d=40μm, D=45 μm.

Accordingly, a rather high GMI ratio of about 400 % is observed even in as-prepared sample (see Figure 2). The highest GMI ratio, $\Delta Z/Z_{max}$, (≈400 %) is observed at f=200 MHz. A double-peak $\Delta Z/Z(H)$ dependence, typical for

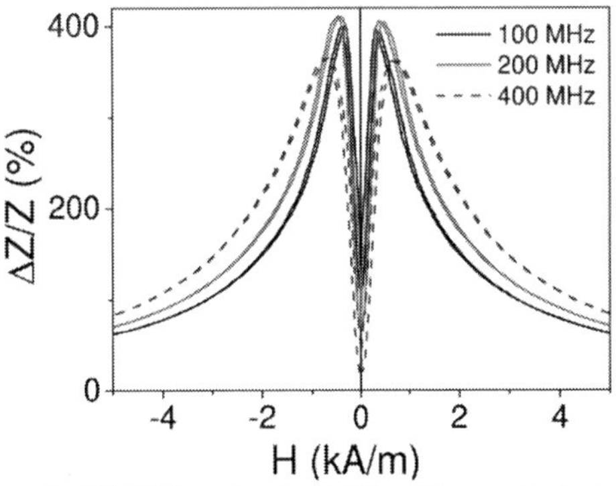

Figure 2. $\Delta Z/Z(H)$ dependencies at different frequencies in studied microwires.

magnetic wires with circumferential magnetic anisotropy [19], is observed at all measured frequencies (see Figure 2). Such features of the GMI effect correlate with the hysteresis loop, particularly with low H_c and H_k -values.

Previously, substantial improvement of the GMI effect was observed after annealing at 300 °C [12]. Therefore, we studied the effect of annealing at 300 °C on hysteresis loops, $\Delta Z/Z_{max}$, and $\Delta Z/Z(H)$ dependence of the studied microwire. The evolution of the hysteresis loops of $Co_{72}Fe_4B_{13}Si_{11}$ microwire after the annealing at T_{ann} =300 °C (60 min) is provided in Figure 3. The main change of the hysteresis loops consists of a decrease in H_k –value up to H_k≈75 A/m, while the H_c remains almost unchanged (H_c≈24 A/m).

The $\Delta Z/Z(H)$ dependencies measured in annealed $Co_{72}Fe_4B_{13}Si_{11}$ microwire are shown in Figure 4. Compared to the as-prepared $Co_{72}Fe_4B_{13}Si_{11}$ microwire, a substantial increase in $\Delta Z/Z_{max}$ –values is observed in the annealed samples. Similarly to the as-prepared $Co_{72}Fe_4B_{13}Si_{11}$ sample, the $\Delta Z/Z(H)$ dependences of annealed $Co_{72}Fe_4B_{13}Si_{11}$

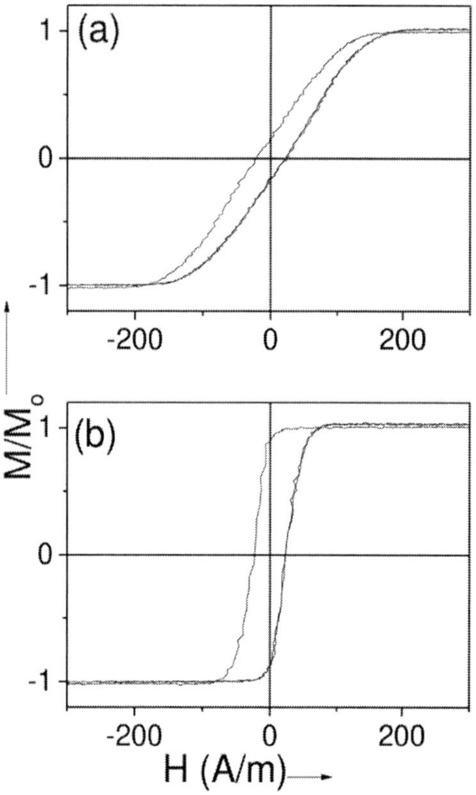

Figure 3. Hysteresis loops of as-prepared (a) and annealed at T_{ann}= = 300 °C (b) $Co_{72}Fe_4B_{13}Si_{11}$ sample.

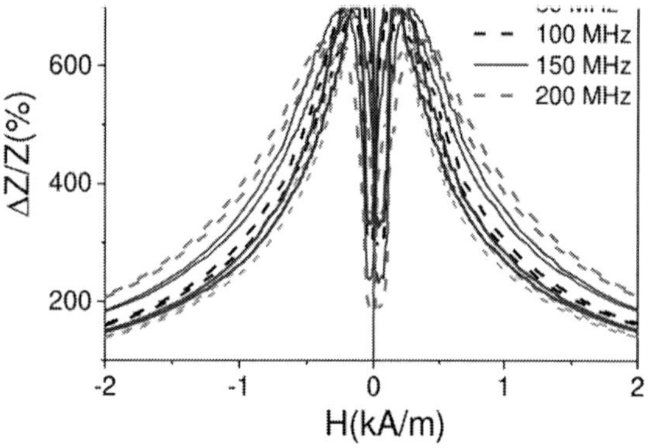

Figure 4. $\Delta Z/Z(H)$ dependencies measured in annealed at 300 °C sample measured at frequencies 70-200 MHz.

microwires have a two-peak character. However, the difference is that the magnetic field H_m, at which $\Delta Z/Z_{max}$ is observed, becomes lower. Thus, for f=100 MHz H_m decreases from 0.35kA/m (for as-prepared sample) to 0.15 kA/m (for all annealed $Co_{72}Fe_4B_{13}Si_{11}$ samples). The magnetic field of maximum, H_m, in $\Delta Z/Z(H)$ dependencies is commonly associated with the magnetic anisotropy field [4][19]. Therefore, the observed change in $\Delta Z/Z(H)$ dependencies after annealing correlates with the evolution of the hysteresis loops upon annealing. On the other hand, higher $\Delta Z/Z_{max}$ –values, observed in annealed $Co_{72}Fe_4B_{13}Si_{11}$ samples must be related to a decrease in magnetic anisotropy field after annealing and internal stresses relaxation.

As observed in Figure 3, the change in the hysteresis loops of the studied microwire towards an increase in the remanent magnetization, M_r/M_0, after annealing is similar to that previously observed for various Co-rich [20]. Such behavior was discussed in terms of the relationship between the λ_s-value, the internal stresses relaxation and the structural relaxation [20]. The characteristic feature of studied glass-coated microwires is the elevated internal stresses related to the preparation method involving rapid solidification of the metallic alloy inside the glass tube [9][10][21]. It has been theoretically predicted and shown experimentally (i.e., by the glass etching) that the largest component of such internal stresses, associated with the difference in the thermal expansion coefficients of the metal alloy and glass, is axial [9][10][22]. Accordingly, a negative λ_s-value, together with the axial character of internal stresses, leads to the transverse magnetic anisotropy of Co-rich microwires with vanishing and negative λ_s, as shown in Figure 3.

Our measurements show that after annealing there is a change in the λ_s-value from low negative (λ_s-≈-9x10^{-7}) to low positive (λ_s-≈11x10^{-7}). Such changes in the λ_s-value can explain the change in the hysteresis loops and the $\Delta Z/Z(H)$ dependencies.

The double-peak $\Delta Z/Z(H)$ dependencies observed for all annealed $Co_{72}Fe_4B_{13}Si_{11}$ sample (see Figure 4) suggest the presence of the transverse magnetic anisotropy in the surface layer of the studied microwires. It looks surprising considering low positive λ_s. The origin of such weak transverse anisotropy on the surface of the studied microwire can be attributed to the presence of an interface layer between the metal core and the glass coating and, consequently, a different chemical composition in the thin surface interface layer. Such an interface layer was previously observed experimentally [23].

IV. CONCLUSIONS

We showed that the GMI effect of Co-rich amorphous magnetic microwires can be substantially improved by appropriate annealing. Quite a high maximum GMI ratio (up to 735%) is observed after annealing of Co-rich microwires. The effect of annealing is discussed in terms of internal stresses relaxation, a change in the magnetostriction coefficient sign and the value upon annealing. Weak transverse magnetic anisotropy evidenced from the obtained hysteresis loops by the shape of $\Delta Z/Z(H)$ dependencies is explained by the presence of the interface layer between the metallic nucleus and the glass-coating.

ACKNOWLEDGMENT

This work was supported by EU under "INFINITE" (HORIZON-CL5-2021-D5-01-06) and "Harmony" (HORIZON-CL4-2023-RESILIENCE-01) projects, by the Spanish MICIN, under PID2022-141373NB-I00 project, by the Government of the Basque Country under PUE_2021_1_0009, Elkartek (MOSINCO and ATLANTIS) projects and under the scheme of "Ayuda a Grupos Consolidados" (ref. IT1670-22). The authors thank the technical and human support provided by SGIker of UPV/EHU (Medidas Magneticas Gipuzkoa) and European funding (ERDF and ESF).

REFERENCES

[1] J. Durand, "Magnetic Properties of Metallic Glasses" in Topics in Applied Physics, vol. 53, 1983, Glassy Metals II. Atomic Structure and Dynamics, Electronic Structure, Magnetic Properties, Editors: H. Beck and H. -J. Giintherodt, Springer-Verlag, Berlin, Heidelberg, New York, Tokyo.

[2] M. Hagiwara, A. Inoue, and T. Masumoto, "Mechanical properties of Fe–Si–B amorphous wires produced by in-rotating-water spinning method", Metall. Trans. A, vol. 13, pp. 373-382, 1982.

[3] D. C. Jiles, "Recent advances and future directions in magnetic materials", Acta Mater., vol. 51, pp. 5907-5939, 2003.

[4] K. Mohri, F. B. Humphrey, K. Kawashima, K. Kimura, and M. Muzutani, "Large Barkhausen and Matteucci effects in FeCoSiB, FeCrSiB, and FeNiSiB amorphous wires", IEEE Trans. Magn., vol. 26, pp. 1789-1781, 1990.

[5] M. Knobel, M. Vazquez, and L. Kraus, "Giant magnetoimpedance", Handbook Magn. Mater., vol. 15, pp. 497- 563, 2003.

[6] A. Zhukov et al., "Giant magnetoimpedance in rapidly quenched materials," J. Alloy Compd., vol. 814, p. 152225, 2020.

[7] K. R. Pirota, L. Kraus, H. Chiriac, and M. Knobel, "Magnetic properties and GMI in a CoFeSiB glass-covered microwire", J. Magn. Magn. Mater., vol. 21, pp. L243-L247, 2000.

[8] P. Corte-León et al., "Engineering of magnetic properties of Co-rich microwires by joule heating", Intermetallics, vol. 105, pp. 92-98, 2019.

[9] H. Chiriac, N. Lupu, G. Stoian, G. Ababei, S. Corodeanu, and T.-A. Óvári, "Ultrathin Nanocrystalline Magnetic Wires", Crystals, vol. 7, p. 48, 2017.

[10] S. A. Baranov, V.S. Larin, and A.V. Torcunov, "Technology, Preparation and Properties of the CastGlass-Coated Magnetic Microwires" Crystals, vol. 7, p. 136, 2017.

[11] D. Kozejova et al., "Biomedical applications of glass-coated microwires", J. Magn. Magn. Mater., vol. 470, pp. 2-5, 2019.

[12] P. Corte-Leon et al., "The effect of annealing on magnetic properties of "Thick" microwires", J.Alloys Compound., vol. 831, p. 150992, 2020.

[13] A. V. Ulitovsky, I. M. Maianski, and A. I. Avramenco, "Method of continuous casting of glass coated microwire", USSR Patent, No. 128427, 1960, Bulletin No. 10, p. 14.

[14] L. Kraus, J. Schneider, and H. Wiesner, "Ferromagnetic resonance in amorphous alloys prepared by rapid quenching from the melt", Czech. J. Phys. B, vol. 26, pp.601–602, 1976.

[15] Y. Konno and K. Mohri, "Magnetostriction measurements for amorphous wires", IEEE Trans Magn., vol. 25, pp. 3623-3625, 1989.

[16] M. Churyukanova et al., "Magnetostriction investigation of soft magnetic microwires", Phys. Stat. Sol. A, vol. 213(2), pp. 363–367, 2016.

[17] L. Gonzalez-Legarreta et al., "Optimization of magnetic properties and GMI effect of Thin Co-rich Microwires for GMI Microsensors", Sensors, vol. 20, p. 1558, 2020.

[18] A. Zhukov et al., "Routes for Optimization of Giant Magnetoimpedance Effect in Magnetic Microwires", IEEE Instrum. Meas. Mag., vol. 23(1), pp. 56-63, 2020.

[19] N. A. Usov, A.S. Antonov, and A.N. Lagar`kov, "Theory of giant magneto-impedance effect in amorphous wires with different types of magnetic anisotropy", J. Magn. Magn. Mater., vol. 185, pp. 159-173, 1998.

[20] A. Zhukov et al., "Engineering of magnetic properties and GMI effect in Co-rich amorphous microwires", J. Alloys and Compounds, vol. 664, pp. 235–241, 2016.

[21] A. Zhukov et al., "Advanced functional magnetic microwires for technological applications", J. Phys. D: Appl. Phys. vol. 55, p. 253003, 2022.

[22] A. S. Antonov, V. T. Borisov, O. V. Borisov, A. F. Prokoshin, and N. A. Usov, "Residual quenching stresses in glass-coated amorphous ferromagnetic microwires", J. Phys. D: Appl. Phys., vol. 33, pp. 1161-1168, 2000.

[23] A. Zhukov et al., "Studies of interfacial layer and its effect on magnetic properties of glass-coated microwires", J. Electr. Mater. vol. 45(5), pp. 2381-2387, 2016.

Magnetic Steel Health Monitoring in the Nano-Scale

Angeliki Mpaliou[1], Tatiana Damatopoulou[1], Spyros Angelopoulos[1], Petros Tsakiridis[1], Gregory Doumenis[2], and Evangelos Hristoforou[1]
[1]Laboratory of Electronic Sensors, National Technical University of Athens, Zografou Campus, Athens 15780, Greece
[2] Department of Informatics and Telecommunications, University of Ioannina, Ioannina 47150, Greece
e-mail: damatat5@yahoo.gr

Abstract— **In this paper, we demonstrate the first trial to perform steel health monitoring inside the steel grain, by comparing the misorientation of the Kikuchi lines with magnetic properties, namely the Barkhausen noise (BHN), differential magnetic permeability and coercivity. The results illustrate monotonic dependence on the magnetic properties on the crystalline misorientation. Apart from that, micro-hardness studies have also been realized, illustrating a monotonic dependence on magnetic properties. Such monotonic dependence allows for the correlation of magnetic properties on mechanical properties and residual stresses and their corresponding use for industrial applications towards steel health monitoring.**

Keywords: Residual stresses; electron back scattering; Barkhausen noise; magnetization loop.

I. Introduction

Magnetization process is evidently dependent on the structure and microstructure of the magnetic substance [1]. The presence of dislocations and nano-precipitates affects both magnetic domain wall mobility and magnetic domain rotation [2]. Thus, magnetic properties, such as M-H loops, Barkhausen noise (BHN), the Magneto-Acoustic Emission (MAE) and the surface magnetic permeability of steels are dependent on the presence of sub-grains, plastic deformation and the size & distribution of nano-precipitates in the grain: they are the reason of residual stresses and mechanical properties, such as hardness and microhardness [3]. The dependence of the magnetic properties on the microstructure is modeled with respect to the dependence of domain wall motion and domain rotation on dislocations and nano-precipitates [4].

We have worked for a long time to develop methodologies and technology to determine residual stresses in the mesoscopic level. This has been achieved by considering residual stresses as an average among a number of grains in ferrous steels [5]. Such analysis has contributed to the quality control of production lines related to steel production and manufacturing, as well as to steel end users. Therefore, it allowed for the actual determination of the distribution of the residual stress tensor on the surface and in the bulk of the ferromagnetic steel [6].

However, the technology up to now has been limited to an average minimum volume of stress detection in the order of 10 cm^3 [7]. The motivation of the current work has been the initiation of studies related to the correlation between magnetic properties and misalignment of the crystalline structure within the grains of magnetic steels. Such a correlation may result in indirect determination of microstrain distribution, anisotropy change and localized microhardness determination within the steel grain.

The materials and methods used are described in Chapter II, followed by experimental analysis using Electron Back Scattering Diffraction (EBSD) studies (Chapter III). Then, a new type of sensor is proposed to precisely monitor residual stresses in minimized surfaces (Chapter IV). Finally, a new method for generating residual stresses in a steel coupon is discussed, offering significant advances in the amplitude of the developed residual stresses in the steel samples (Chapter V).

II. Materials and Methods

Armco steel, with less than 7 ppm carbon and 5 ppm sulfur, has been chosen as the type of steel to initiate this type of measurements, due to its single phase ferritic structure, similar to the electric steel structure. Armco steel samples have been cold-rolled up to 65% reduction of cross section and then they have been properly polished to undergo EBSD, using Struers polishing instrumentation [8]. EBSD studies were realized using a JEOL 6380LV scanning electron microscope, equipped with a Thermo Fisher Scientific EBSD instrumentation to determine the misalignment of Kikuchi lines inside the grains and therefore to determine the degree of misorientation of the crystalline structure in the grains of the Armco steel. The polished Armco samples, as well as Armco samples directly after cold rolling, have been used to determine their magnetic properties. Two different magnetic measurements have been realized, namely Barkhausen noise (BHN) [9], as well as M-H hysteresis loop measurements [10]. The BHN measurements were realized by the MEB 2c instrument from Mag-Lab sc; Gdansk, Poland [11]. M-H loop measurements were realized by a home-made set-up employing a Kethley signal generator, a KEPCO current amplifier, an MFLI Lock-in Amplifier, and an Agilent 200 MHz oscilloscope. BHN measurements offered the local number of Barkhausen jumps and the BHN envelope, while the M-H loops offered the local coercivity H_c and remanence M_R, at the region of measurements.

Finally, microhardness measurements have been realized using the facilities of the Research and Standardization Centre of the Power Public Corporation of Greece.

III. Experimental Results

The grain misorientation is illustrated by means of pole figures of EBSD (Figure 1), following the Thermo Fischer Scientific calculations based on the Kikuchi lines determination in sub-micron regions. Misorientation was found to be enhanced with respect to cold rolling process, as expected. The dependence of misorientation angle of the grains on the cold rolling reduction is illustrated in Figure 2. Apart from that, misorientation angle was also correlated with microhardness of the cold rolled Armoco steel, as illustrated in Figure 3. Following the EBSD characterization, BHN measurements were realized, by means of mapping the whole surface of the Armco steel. Figure 4 illustrates a typical response of BHN mapping under different reduction percentages.

The correlation between BHN measurements was realized with respect to microhardness measurements: BHN envelop and microhardness dependence on cross section reduction is illustrated in Figure 5. The systematic monotonic tendency can be seen, with a rather large uncertainty, due to the mismatching in the pointed microhardness and BHN measurements. The correlation between magnetic properties determined by the M-H loop illustrates significantly better uncertainty, due to the more averaging nature of the method. A typical dependence of the coercive field on the EBSD-determined misorientation angle is illustrated in Figure 6.

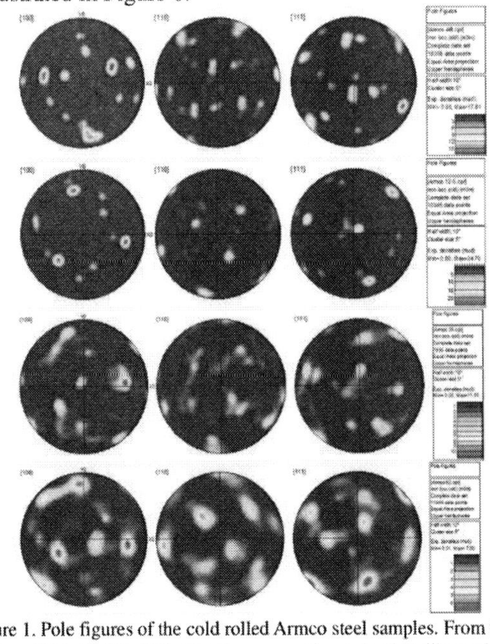

Figure 1. Pole figures of the cold rolled Armco steel samples. From top to bottom: 25%, 12,5%, 50%, 62,5% cross section reduction, illustrating an increase of misorientation with cross section decrease.

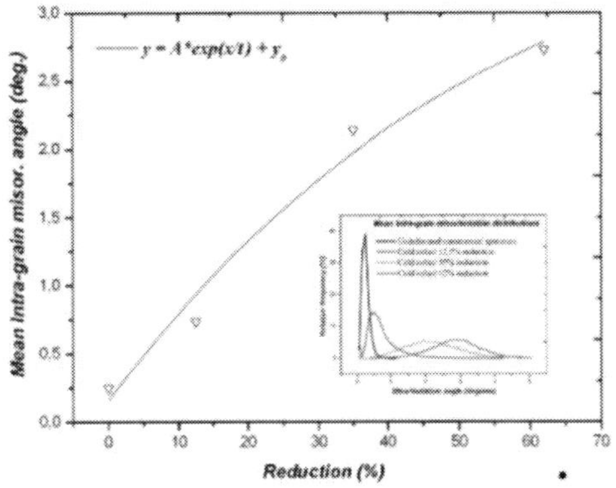

Figure 2. Dependence of the misorientation angle on the reduction % of the Armco steel.

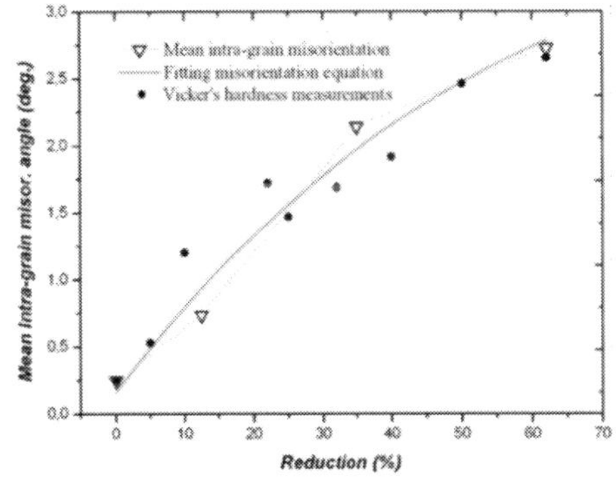

Figure 3. Comparison of the mean intra-grain misorientation angle and the Vicker's hardness in different cross section reduction.

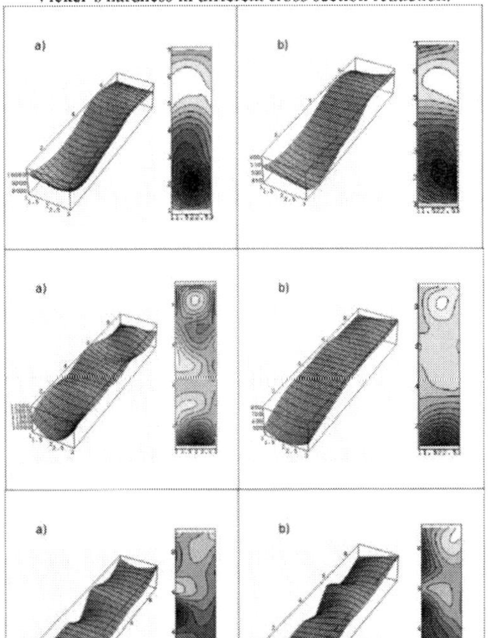

Figure 4. BHN mapping on the surface of cold rolled Armco steel. BHN counts are represented in (a) and BHN envelop is represented in (b). Top: 25% cold rolling. Middle: 50% cold rolling. Bottom: 62,5% cold rolling.

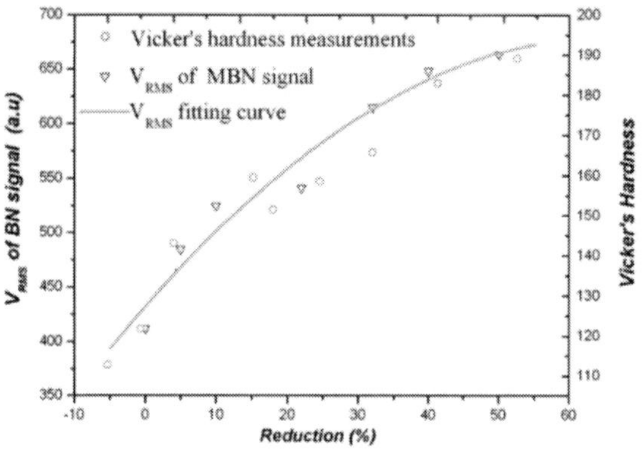

Figure 5. Dependence of BHN envelop and microhardness on the cross section reduction of the Armco steel.

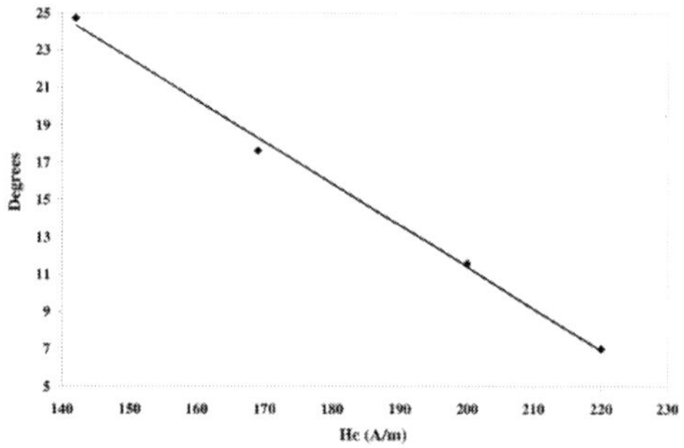

Figure 6. Typical dependence of the crystalline misorientation angle in a sum of grains in the Armco steel on the average coercive field in the same area.

Furthermore, the dependence of the remanence magnetization M_R on the microhardness of the Armco steel samples is illustrated in Figure 7. A clear monotonic dependence with lower uncertainty is observable.

Magnetic measurements of the cold rolled Armco steel were realized not only after polishing the cold rolled samples, but also directly after cross section reduction, illustrating almost the same behavior. This means that the surface roughness of the cold rolled samples is not an issue for hard measurements, this allowing for easier industrial use of the method.

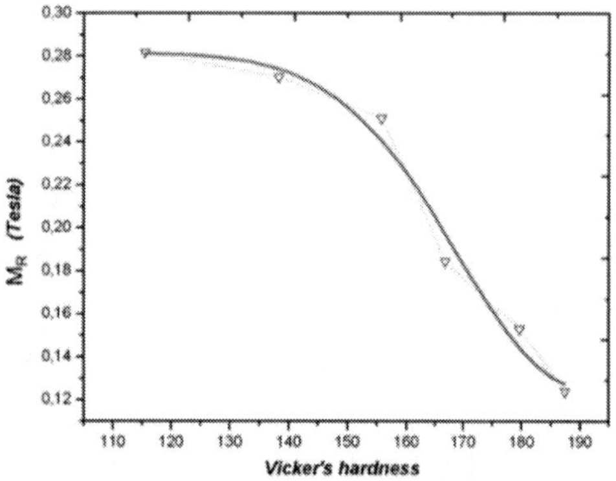

Figure 7. Dependence of the remanence magnetization M_R on the Vicker's hardness.

A similar type of magnetic measurements, employing the determination of the differential magnetic permeability in different types of steels, including Armco steel, have also been realized, illustrating a similar, or even more sensitive, characterization tool [12]. The above mentioned magnetic techniques can be employed to determine the level of plastic deformation of steels, thus improving the existing state of the art in steel non-destructive testing for the plastic deformation region, offering the possibility of early stage steel structural health monitoring. The most straightforward result from the illustrated experimental results is that the grain misorientation angle of cold rolled ferritic steel samples is monotonically dependent on the cross section reduction and the magnetic properties of the steel.

Furthermore, the application-oriented interesting result is the monotonic dependence of macroscopic magnetic properties on the Armco steel microhardness. The dependence of coercivity and remamence on microhardness is clearly demonstrating the ability of M-H characterization to operate as a microhardness determination tool. Since it is a non-destructive approach, the ease of measurement allows for practical industrial and field application. Bearing in mind the similarity of the Armco steel with electric steels, which have the same microstructure as Armco steel, the methodology and technology presented in this article can be used for the characterization of electric steel, which opens a new era in faster and non-destructive characterization of electric steels, with so important applications in our days, namely their use in electric vehicles. This fact is considered as a significant add-on the technology of electric steel (and ferritic steel in general) non-destructive characterization. The thermal stamping of these steels to develop either stators or rotors, results in residual stresses, thus affecting the magnetic permeability and thus the performance of the electric motors. The classical method of annihilating such stresses and corresponding recovery of magnetic properties of these stators and rotors is the heat annealing of the whole stator or rotor. This may result in mechanical softening of the rest of the electric steel, instead of the cutting region only. Using such localized stress measurements, stress annihilation and therefore permeability optimization can be realized, only in the region of elevated residual stresses, using localized RF induction heating at ranges of excitation current, corresponding to the level of residual stresses.

However, these are the first results of magnetic steel structural health monitoring in the nanoscale, related to a single phase magnetic steel. In order to actually evaluate the ability of magnetic measurements to offer monotonic dependence on multiphase ferromagnetic steels, including low carbon steels (carbides), austenitic steels suffering martensitic transformation, dual or multi-phase steels like Duplex steels, or even high entropy alloys demonstrating magnetic properties, a systematic work on such characterization is required. Such work must be realized most probably in an inter-laboratory comparison procedure, since it is important for the steel industry in total: it reduces the cost and the time for quality control of the under test steel, permitting total quality control in all steel production and manufacturing due to its non-destructive character. But all magnetic measurements presented in this work, even the BHN measurements refer to at least a mm^2 surface measuremen, thus averaging a vast number of grains in terms of magnetic measurements. Therefore, a magnetic method to provide magnetic measurements with the same spatial resolution is needed, to take full advantage of the method. The existing state of the art in such technology is the magnetic force microscopy (MFM), allowing for a very similar spatial resolution in comparison to the EBSD method [13]. Of course, the MFM technology cannot be industrially used. For this reason, an industrially applicable method and technology is required to achieve measurements with a spatial resolution in the order of micrometers. Such a sensor is presented in the next session of this work.

IV. A MICRO SIZED PERMEABILITY SENSOR

The principle of such a microsensor is depicted in Figure 8. The sensor offers spatial resolution in the order of μm, with a sampling rate in the order of μs [14]. Pulsed current is transmitted to the thin film pulsed current conductor, which splits into two thin film pulsed current conductors of the same dimensions, thus being able to transmit the same amount of current through them. A thin film magnetic field layer is set between the two pulsed current conductors, able to monitor magnetic field along its surface. Two insulating thin films are used to separate the thin magnetic film from the two thin film pulsed current conductors. The external side of the thin film pulsed current conductor accommodates the sensor electronics, including its stored calibration data, preferably in the form of application-specific-integrated-circuit (ASIC). The external side of the thin film pulsed current conductor accommodates the thin film external packaging of the sensor, which can attach the surface of the ferromagnetic steel under measurement.

An electronic circuit, preferably embedded in the sensor and the mentioned ASIC is used to wirelessly transfer the data of the sensor. A position sensor, indicatively being a photonic sensor, like those operating in the mouse of a personal computer, or even an interferometer, is used for monitoring the position of the magnetic thin film, the output of which is connected to the electronic circuit, thus wirelessly transferring the position data of the sensor. The operation of the sensor is as follows: the thin film external packaging of the sensor touches the surface under measurement and the output of the thin magnetic film is monotonically dependent on the surface permeability and the residual stresses of the surface area of the steel under measurement, defined by the projection of the surface of the thin magnetic film. These data in the form of stress components and positions are transmitted to a portable computer or tablet or smartphone, offering the mapping of the surface stress tensor distribution by using the in-house application-specific-software.

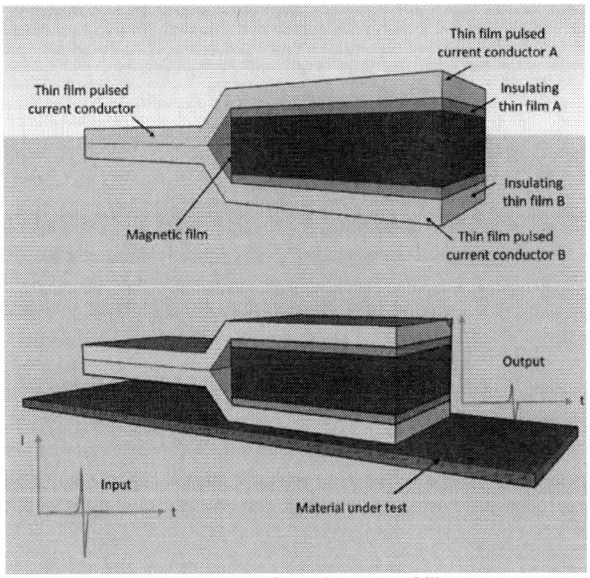

Figure 8. The new microsensor for surface permeability measurements (top) and its operation (bottom)

When pulsed current is transmitted through the two pulsed current conductors, they generate magnetic field parallel to their surface, which penetrates the thin film magnetic sensor. The fields H_1 and H_2 from the two pulsed current conductors are proportional to the transmitted pulsed currents I_1 & I_2 to each one of them, and inversely proportional to the distance d_1 & d_2 between the said pulsed current conductors and the thin magnetic film:

$$H_1 = a\frac{I_1}{d_1} \qquad (1)$$

And

$$H_2 = -a\frac{I_2}{d_2} \qquad (2)$$

Where a, is a proportionality constant. Considering the pulsed currents I_1 & I_2 equal each other and the distances d_1 & d_2 equal each other then, the total field H along the surface of the thin magnetic film is:

$$H = H_1 + H_2 = a\frac{I}{d} + \left(-a\frac{I}{d}\right) = 0 \quad (3)$$

Thus, the output of the thin film sensor equals zero and corresponds to its zero reference field.

When the sensor, and particularly the packaging part of it approaches the ferromagnetic steel under measurement, provided that the distance between the packaging part of the sensor and the ferromagnetic steel is small (in the order of a few μm), the magnetic lines due to the field H_1 are partially trapped by the ferromagnetic steel under measurement, allowing only a part of the magnetic field H_1 to remain in the volume of the thin magnetic film:

$$H_1 = H_1 - H_1^{\mu} \quad (4)$$

Where H_1^{μ} is the magnetic field corresponding to the magnetic lines trapped by the surface of the ferromagnetic steel under measurement, which are dependent on the surface permeability of it. Instead, most of the magnetic lines due to the field H_2 remain in the area close to the thin magnetic film according to Maxwell equations. Therefore, an imbalance in the magnetic field within the volume of the thin magnetic film is generated and H becomes:

$$H = -H_1^{\mu} \quad (5)$$

Therefore, the output of the thin magnetic film is proportional to the surface permeability component of the ferromagnetic steel under measurement, parallel to the magnetic fields H_1 & H_2. It is also known that the permeability component μ of a ferromagnetic steel is proportional to the residual stress component σ in the area of its surface and the corresponding direction or in a corresponding volume just below it:

$$\sigma = b\mu \text{ or } \sigma_x = b\mu_x \;\&\; \sigma_y = b\mu_y \quad (6)$$

Therefore, the output of the thin magnetic film is proportional to the stress component parallel to the magnetic fields H_1 & H_2. Change of orientation of the sensor or manufacturing of several sensors in the same chip, in corresponding directions, offers the ability of monitoring the stress components on the surface of the ferromagnetic steel under measurement. The thin magnetic film can be in any of the existing, industrially available thin magnetic film field sensors, namely anisotropic magnetoresistance (AMR) sensors, giant magnetoresistive (GMR) sensors, spin valve sensors, etc. The largest surface of these sensors, currently available in the market of ASIC, like permalloy films, is far below 100 μm X 100 μm, while the surface of 1 μm X 1 μm thin film magnetic field sensor is easily achievable in the form of AMR arrangement following classical microelectronics technology. Thus, the special resolution of the sensor can easily be in the order of 1 μm^2. Apart from that the excitation and the reading ability of electronics can be less than 1 μs, thus allowing for single point measurements in less than 1 point per 1 μs. The sensitivity and uncertainty of the stress sensor are dependent on the sensitivity and uncertainty of the implemented thin film magnetic field sensor. Bearing in mind that the worst sensitivity of the above mentioned thin film magnetic field sensors (AMR, GMR etc.) is 1 nT@$Hz^{-1/2}$, the sensitivity of the sensor in pulsed operation is better than 1 nT. Motion of the sensor along the surface of the ferromagnetic steel under measurement, and use of the data from the position sensor offers the dependence of the stress components on the different areas of the surface of the ferromagnetic steel under measurement.

V. DISCUSSION

This type of magnetic measurement can be realized in electric steel production manufacturing lines. The new era of electric motion requires significantly advanced cores for stators and rotors, thus permitting reduction of size and weight of electric motors. The methodology and technology presented in this paper can be used for microstructural characterization and mechanical properties determination, both being important for the proper quality control of the produced electric steel. Therefore, a robotic system based on the measuring methods presented in this paper, the total quality control of the whole electric steel production can be realized, thus offering a significant advantage to the electric steel producers following the methodology. Furthermore, the electric steel manufacturers, using hot stamping technology to develop parts of the stator and rotor of electric machines can also use this technology in order to locally annihilate the electric steel at the surfaces of stamping, by using localized induction heating. An example of such treatment is illustrated in Figure 9, where a simple RF heater with point high frequency conductors can be used to locally apply eddy currents and correspondingly generate localized heat in the material. Due to the relatively low thermal conductivity of steels, heat is rather concentrated in the area of eddy currents, allowing for localized stress annihilation process. Experiments have also been realized in oriented and non-oriented electric steel sheets, which have undergone localized heating and consequent quenching (Figure 10). Temperature was elevated up to 300°C and 500°C with consequent quenching with water. The quenched areas of the surface of the steel sheets can be seen by naked eye. After quenching, thermal treatment resulted in annihilating residual stresses for the case of 300°C. However, such annihilation was not achievable for the case of 500°C heated and consequently quenched electric steel sheet.

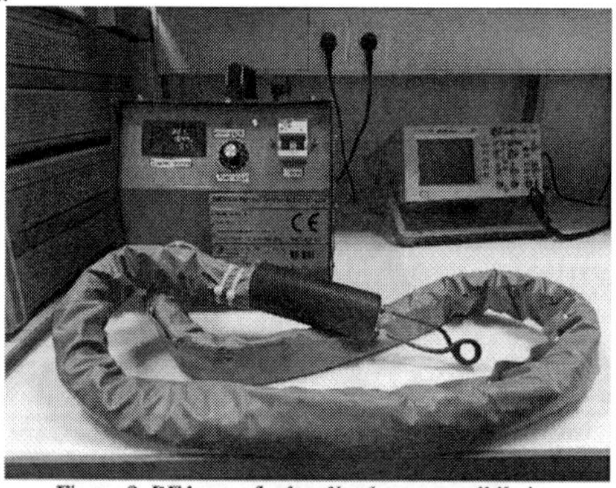

Figure 9. RF heater for localized stress annihilation

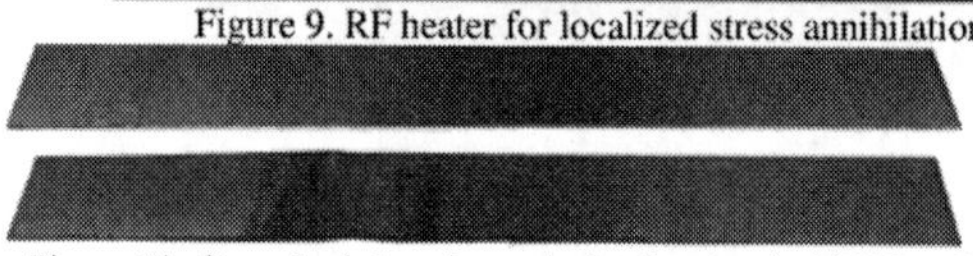

Figure 10. Quenched electric steel after heating in 300°C and 500°C. The quenched areas can be seen by naked eye.

The same principle can also be used for determination of the magnetic stress calibration (MASC) curve in steels [6], allowing for the proper development of data for the calibration of residual stress determination of steel sheets. Future work has already been initiated for this purpose, requiring additional inter-laboratory tests to verify the level of uncertainty of measurements. An example of such a MASC based on the RF induction heating and consequent quenching is illustrated in Figure 11, for electric steel and 42CrMo4 steel. These measurements have been determined using an AMR sensor, with direct correlation of the AMR output in μT with residual stresses in MPa. Such a response is enhanced with respect to our previous method for the determination of MASC curve, using welded samples, for several reasons, the most important being the maintenance of the steel phase. However, even the use of this technique, named 3MA technique, suffers from the problem of not being able to recon between positive and negative magnetostrictive ematerials. This issue is overcome by using our patented microsensor. The nature of manufacturing this type of sensor allows for the development of two sensors with 90° shift, thus allowing simultaneous measurement of two directions, resulting in the determination of surface permeability in both axes, which may be used for determination of the effective field caused by positive and negative magnetostriction. Results based on this principle are illustrated in Figure 12, where the measurement of localized stresses can be seen for the case of a non-oriented electric steel sheet, heated and water-quenched in 500°C. Such a response demonstrates the main principle of innovation presented in this paper.

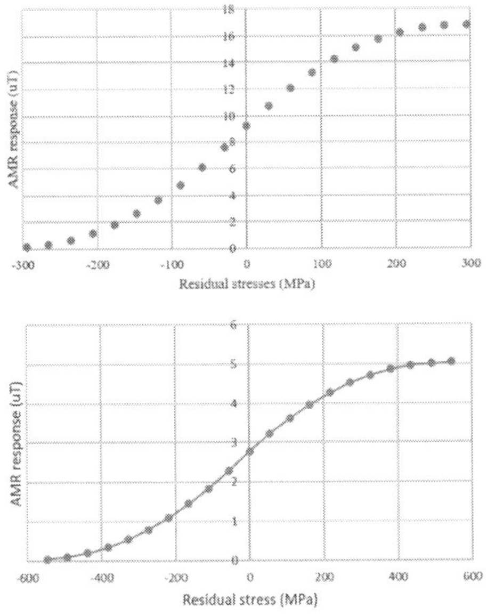

Figure 11. New MASC curves based on the RF induction method. Top: Electric Steel MASC curve. Bottom: 42CrMo4 steel MASC curve.

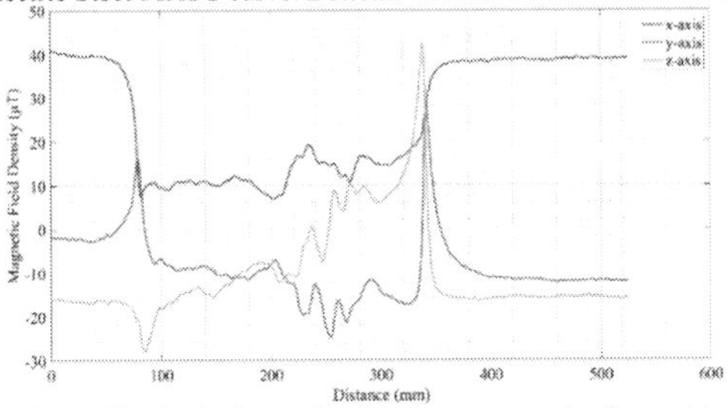

Figure 12. Monitoring residual stresses as a result of quenching in NOES.

VI. Conclusions

A non-destructive method for the determination of the micro-structural misorientation in cold rolled Armco ferritic steels has been presented in this article. Apart from that, the presented methodology allows for the determination of hardness in this type of steel. All measurements demonstrate a monotonic dependence of magnetic properties on the misorientation angle and microhardness of plastically deformed samples. A new, patented, type of sensor has also been presented, able to detect surface magnetic permeability with spatial resolution in the order of μm^2. Finally, a new method for developing residual stresses in steels is also proposed, allowing for easier inter-laboratory comparison tests with better levels of uncertainties. Future work, based on these inter-laboratory tests is required to achieve the initial work for the preparation of a related Standard of residual stress measurements and their correlation with magnetic properties.

Acknowledgment

This work was supported by the European Union and Greek National Funds through the Operational Program Competitiveness, Entrepreneurship and Innovation, under the call RESEARCH-CREATE-INNOVATE under Project T2EDK-02521.

References

[1] J. M. D. Coey, "Magnetism and magnetic materials", Cambridge University Press, 2010

[2] S. Takahashi, J. Echigoya, and Z. Motoki, "Magnetization curves of plastically deformed Fe metals and alloys", *J. Appl. Phys.* 87, 805–813 (2000), https://doi.org/10.1063/1.371945

[3] I. Altpeter, G. Dobmann, M. Kröning, M. Rabung, and S. Szielasko, "Micro-magnetic evaluation of micro residual stresses of the IInd and IIIrd order", NDT & E International 42 (4), 283-290, 2009

[4] E. Olivetti, F. Fiorillo, E. Forton, L. Martino, and L. Rocchino, "Microstructure and magnetic properties of pure iron for cyclotron electromagnets", Journal of Alloys and Compounds, 615, Pages S291-S295, 2014

[5] P. Vourna, A. Ktena, P. Tsakiridis, and E. Hristoforou, "A novel approach of accurately evaluating residual stress and microstructure of welded electrical steels", NDT and E International 71, pp. 33-42, 2015

[6] E. Hristoforou, P. Vourna, A. Ktena, and P. Svec, "On the Universality of the Dependence of Magnetic Parameters on Residual Stresses in Steels", IEEE Transactions on Magnetics 52(5),7362189, 2016

[7] A. Ktena, E. Hristoforou, "Stress dependent magnetization and vector preisach modeling in low carbon steels", IEEE Transactions on Magnetics 48 (4), 1433-1436, 2012

[8] D. J. Dingley, V. Randle, "Microtexture determination by electron back-scatter diffraction". J Mater Sci, 27, pp. 4545–4566, 1992

[9] D. Spasojević, S. Bukvić, S. Milošević, and H. Eugene Stanley, "Barkhausen noise: Elementary signals, power laws, and scaling relations", Phys. Rev. E. 54, 2531-2546, 1996

[10] D. L. Atherton, D. C. Jiles, "Effects of stress on magnetization", NDT international 19.1, 15-19, 1986

[11] L. Piotrowski, B. Augustyniak, M. Chmielewski, E. V. Hristoforou, and K. Kosmas, "Evaluation of Barkhausen Noise and Magnetoacoustic Emission Signals Properties for Plastically Deformed Armco Iron," *IEEE Transactions on Magnetics*, 46, 239-242, 2010

[12] P. Vourna; E. Hristoforou; A. Ktena; P. Svec; and E. Mangiorou, "Dependence of Magnetic Permeability on Residual Stresses in Welded Steels", IEEE Transactions on Magnetics, 53, Article 6200704, 2017

[13] E. Sarantopoulou, S. Kobe, K. Z. Rozman, Z. Kollia, G. Drazic, and A. C. Cefalas, "Fabrication of magnetic SmFe films by pulsed laser deposition at 157 nm", *IEEE Transactions on Magnetics*, 40, pp. 2943-2945, 2004

[14] Multi-layer thin film sensor for non-destructive testing of perromagnetic materials, US Patent, 072517INTEFSW10512900, 2017

Signal-Processing Algorithms for Sensor Arrays: A Brief Review

Sergio Dominguez-Gimeno
Dept. of Electronic Engineering
and Communications
University of Zaragoza
Teruel, Spain
e-mail: sdominguezg@unizar.es

Raul Igual-Catalan
Dept. of Electric Engineering
University of Zaragoza
Teruel, Spain
e-mail: rigual@unizar.es

Inmaculada Plaza-Garcia
Dept. of Electronic Engineering
and Communications
University of Zaragoza
Teruel, Spain
e-mail: inmap@unizar.es

***Abstract*—A sensor array is a special topology of sensors in which all of them fulfill a common function. These sensor arrays have a wide variety of applications and nature. As the signals produced by these arrays highly depend on them, very different processing algorithms can be designed for them. In this paper, a brief review of the families of algorithms that are applied to sensor arrays is given. A total of 171 papers have been analyzed and percentages of usage of each family of algorithms are provided. The algorithms found are very diverse and highly depend on the application of sensor arrays. However, it has been found that very different arrays can accomplish the same task and can be processed in the same way.**

Keywords-sensor array; algorithms; machine learning; numerical methods; review.

I. Introduction

Sensor arrays are arrangements of several sensors in the same device. These arrays are based on different technologies, like resistive arrays [1], capacitive arrays [2], triboelectric arrays [3], piezoelectric arrays [4], etc. This topology allows very diverse applications like aerospace [5], surgery [6][7], gas classification [8], bidimensional pressure distribution sensing [9], or damage monitoring in structures [10]. In this article, special attention is paid to the processing algorithms used to treat the signals the sensor arrays provide. A global classification of the types of algorithms is also provided.

The remainder of the paper is organized as follows: In Section II, the search and selection procedure is explained; in Section III, the algorithms found are classified by families and some examples of use are listed; in Section IV, the results are discussed; and in Section V, some conclusions are drawn.

II. Methods

A systematic search on sensor arrays in the *Web Of Science* (WOS) database is conducted to provide a general vision of the field. In order to cover all possible technologies on sensing arrays, the title keywords searched, together with the number of selected results, are: "Resistive Sensor Array" (RSA, 45 results), "Piezoresistive Sensor Array" (PRSA, 32 results), "Capacitive Sensor Array" (CSA, 57 results), "Inductive Sensor Array" (ISA, 6 results), "Diode Sensor Array" (DSA, 6 results), "Transistor Sensor Array" (TSA, 24 results), "Piezoelectric Sensor Array" (PSA, 66 results), "Triboelectric Sensor Array" (TrSA, 14 results), "Fiber-optic Sensor Array" (FSA, 14 results), "Hall-effect Sensor Array" (HSA, 6 results), and "Bioimpedance Sensor Array" (BSA, 2 results).

Searches were performed in January 2023, and repeated in September 2023. All results from 2016 to September 2023 were taken for analysis. Journals, magazines, and conferences were considered in the searches. A total of 322 papers were found. The title and abstract of each paper was examined and results not related to the aim of this research were discarded. This led to 316 studies. The content of the studies was then examined, discarding those not related to the topic of this review, or those that did not mention the processing algorithms. This lead to a total of 171 papers selected to be deeply analyzed. This is a brief review to study the current state of the art of sensor array processing algorithms.

III. Results

The different families of algorithms found are listed in this section. A summary of them can be seen in Figure 1.

A. Classic signal processing algorithms

1) FFT-based algorithms: The most common technique for frequency analysis is the Fast Fourier Transform (FFT) [11], followed by the Wavelet Transform (WT) [12]. Other techniques are Short-Time FT (STFT) [4], Power Spectral Density (PSD) [2][10][13], the Discrete Cosine Transform (DCT) [14], the Hilbert Transform (HT) [15], and, finally the S-Transform [16]. These are applied works whose sensors have a frequential response, like PSA [14][17], for example, for Structure Health Monitoring (SHM). In [10], the PSD is obtained to calculate a Crack Growth Index (CGI), which allows fatigue sensing in structures. Capacitive Micromachined Ultrasonic Transducers (CMUTs) can be based on CSA, so they must be analyzed in the frequency domain [8]. They can be used to detect Volatile Organic Compounds (VOCs) or Liquids (VOLs). In [18], frequency analysis is used to obtain vibrations of the flexible solar panels of a satellite and compensate them, using a PID algorithm. Zhang et al. [16] assess power transformers isolation through ultrasound signals obtained with a fiber-optic sensor array and processed with the S-Transform. In [19], a HSA for magnetometry is developed and magnetic noise is studied similarly.

2) Tracking algorithms: Several works use algorithms to follow the position of a certain object. In [20], a CSA is used for contact-less hand tracking. In the field of surgery, instruments can be tracked inside the human body using HSA [7]. HSAs are also used in [21] for microrobot position tracking. In [22],

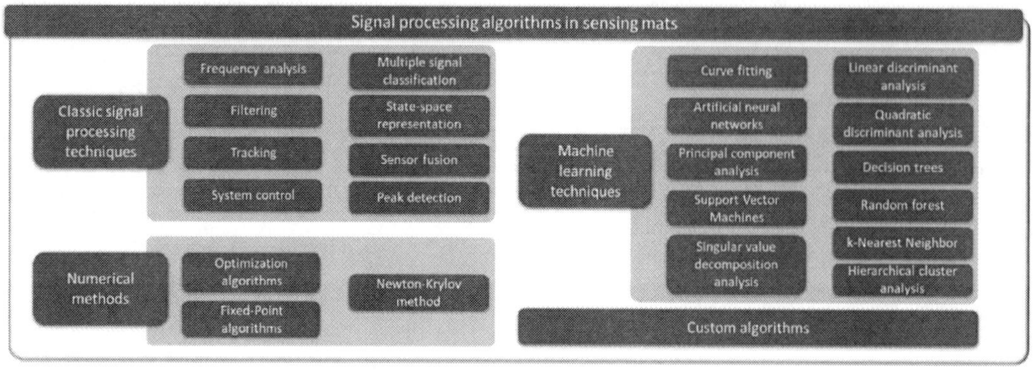

Figure 1. Families of processing algorithms found during this work that are applied for sensor array signal processing.

particle tracking is performed with Time-of-Flight diode-based imaging sensors.

3) Fusion algorithms: It is the combination of the information of different sensors for enhanced sensing. It is common in the field of Inertial Measurement Units (IMUs): signals from the accelerometer, the gyroscope and the magnetometer are combined to compensate for their measurements [23]. In [24], an IMU and a PRSA are combined for smart ping-pong monitoring. The number and type of racket strokes are recorded.

4) Other processing techniques: Digital filtering has also been frequently found due to its importance in sensor post-processing. For example, band-pass and high-pass filters were found to be used to reject AC-power noise [25]. In [26], a radiation waste location system is developed through a FSA. The position readout is refined by applying a Savitzky-Golay filter. Multiple SIgnal Classification (MUSIC) is an algorithm that is applied for SHM using PSA [12]. For vehicle monitoring during aerospace launch, a state-space approach is adopted in [5]. It is performed using an IMU based on FSA. Finally, peak detection in IMU signals is applied in [24] to count the number of strokes with the ping-pong racket.

B. Machine Learning algorithms

Artificial Intelligence (AI) is a current trend in software for all kind of purposes. In this work, applications of different AI techniques to sensor arrays are explained. Machine Learning (ML) and Deep Learning (DL) algorithms found during this research are listed below:

1) Curve fitting: This is the most common technique used in the ML family, found in 31.2% of the articles. It is mainly used to obtain a mathematical relationship between the physical phenomena and the electric signal output of the sensor array. For example, Ko et al. [3] developed a PSA that was able to detect wind speed and direction. It showed a quadratic relationship between the wind speed and its output voltage.

2) Neural Network (NN): Neural Networks are the most popular DL algorithms in all fields, used for regression or classification. NN algorithms have been reported in the field of breathing sensors, for example, for diabetes diagnosis [27], but also in classification of VOCs with PSAs [28], or hand gesture classification with PRSA [29]. Backpropagation NNs, are applied in [17] to detect transverse cracks in railways. Convolutional NNs are used in [13] to obtain the cardiac pulse at the wrist from a BSA. In [30], a PRSA that is able to detect multi-touch points is calibrated with a NN with single-touch signals. PRSA calibration is also performed in [31], in this case, with a Wavelet NN. A different approach is made in [32]: a FET-based physical NN for the prevention of ulcers in bedridden patients is manufactured in standard CMOS.

3) Principal Component Analysis (PCA): A very popular technique to deal with high amounts of data that can help reduce the dimensionality in a problem by analyzing dependencies between considered features. It has been found to be frequently applied in classification of VOCs and VOLs [28]. Yoon et al. [8] use PCA to classify different VOCs through a CSA. They were able to detect Toluene, Acetone, Ethanol and Methanol using only three dimensions.

4) Support Vector Machines (SVM): These allow the expansion of the number of considered classification features. In [29], SVMs show the best classification results for hand gesture recognition among other ML techniques.

5) k-Nearest Neighbor (kNN): This method groups information into classes through a "neighbor voting" system. It is applied for roughness object recognition in [33], with high accuracy. Also used in [24], to classify different types of racket hits. In [34], a non-contact gesture recognition system based on an ISA is proposed. Gestures are classified using kNN, SVM and RF.

6) Hierarchical Cluster Analysis (HCA): This ML algorithm is used in [28] for VOC classification. Clusters are groups created depending on several features of training data. Then, sensed gases are classified into the available clusters.

7) Decision Trees (DT) and Random Forest (RF): A feature-based supervised algorithm of low computational cost. It has been found to be applied within an anti-vandalism system developed with FSA [11]. Also in [33], for robotic finger motion detection and object properties recognition, showing high accuracy.

8) Linear Discriminant Analysis (LDA) and Quadratic Discriminant Analysis (QDA): LDA and QDA are two statistical ML algorithms used in [29] for hand gesture recognition with a PRSA.

9) Singular Value Decompositon Analysis (SVDA): This reduces the amount of data to work with, based in a matrix factorization. It used is in [35] to detect objects immersed in sand using electrical capacitance tomography.

C. Numerical methods (NM)

In [9], Least-Squares (LSQR), Levenberg-Marquardt, Fixed-Point (FP), and Newton-Krylov algorithms are tested for crosstalk correction in RSA. Thus, readout accuracy of RSAs can be increased with post-processing methods [1][36]. LSQR showed the highest accuracy, at the cost of considerable processing time, while FP showed the highest computational speed with reasonable accuracy. Orthogonal Matching Pursuit (OMP) is another optimization greedy search algorithm that is used in [14] for SHM through PSAs. These PSAs are based on sound waves traveling inside the materials, and the OMP reconstruct these signals.

D. Classic statistical techniques

Classic statistical techniques are found in [27] and applied in breathing sensor arrays. For example, Discriminant Factor Analysis can be used to recognize the sensor that performs the best within an array.

E. Custom algorithms

Other algorithms that have not been able to fit into other families are grouped here. A custom image algorithm for damage imaging in a cylindrical pipe is proposed is [37]. In [38], a wind speed and direction detection algorithm is designed for a PRSA. An algorithm that fuses electromagnetic and magnetic signals is applied for Unexploded Ordnance (UXO) detection with an ISA in [39]. This leads to longer detection distances.

IV. Discussion

Processing algorithms sorted by their number of occurrence are represented in Figure 2. Only the most frequent algorithms are shown. FFT is the most popular technique in frequency analysis, closely followed by NN, in AI algorithms. The ML family of algorithms has the highest percentage of use (17.7% total). This is explained as ML classification algorithms, like NN, SVM, PCA, etc. are very versatile and are becoming very popular lately. Frequency analysis (FFT, WT, PSD, etc.) are the second most common techniques (17.3% total), followed by Numerical Methods, as optimization approaches have demonstrated to be very applicable to solve sensor array inaccuracies. The most commonly found technologies in sensor arrays have been PSA and CSA.

FFT-based algorithms (FFT, PSD, WT, etc.) are usually fast and lightweight algorithms that can easily run on any general-purpose PC. However, in embedded systems with few resources, they may run out of RAM. NN-based algorithms require large training data sets and long iterative training-testing processes, but in return they provide high processing speed, mainly when parallelized on Graphics Processing Units (GPUs). NNs are difficult to train in embedded systems due to this fact. Currently,

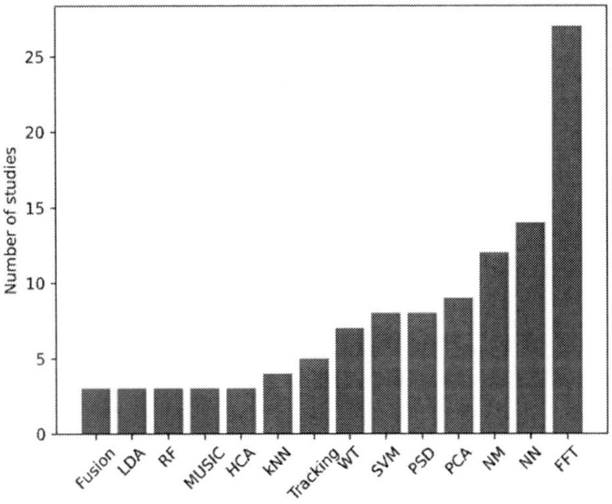

Figure 2. Processing algorithms applied to sensor arrays sorted by the number of occurrences.

NNs perform better than other typical ML algorithms (such as PCA, kNN, HCA, SVM, etc.). However, the latter methods require fewer computer resources because they have fewer parameters.

V. Conclusion and Future Work

Sensor arrays have very diverse applications and, therefore, the processing algorithms applied to them are very varied. Results show that none of the considered families of algorithms is predominant in use. Further research will be conducted in the future to provide a comprehensive view of the entire field. Nowadays, there is a lack of application of modern AI models in various sensor domains. In the coming years, AI is expected to take its place in the field of sensor arrays, making use of neural networks such as Large Language Models. Modelling of non-idealities, sensor design assistance, circuit analysis, didactic tools, etc. can be expected as applications of AI in the near future.

References

[1] J. Martinez-Cesteros, C. Medrano-Sanchez, I. Plaza-Garcia, and R. Igual-Catalan, "Uncertainty analysis in the inverse of equivalent conductance method for dealing with crosstalk in 2-d resistive sensor arrays," *IEEE Sensors Journal*, vol. 22, no. 1, pp. 373–384, 2022. DOI: 10.1109/JSEN.2021.3129668.

[2] W. Gao *et al.*, "A high-resolution mems capacitive force sensor with bionic swallow comb arrays for ultralow multiphysics measurement," *IEEE Transactions on Industrial Electronics*, vol. 70, no. 7, pp. 7467–7477, 2022. DOI: 10.1109/TIE.2022.3203756.

[3] H.-J. Ko, D.-S. Kwon, S. Pyo, and J. Kim, "Curved flap array-based triboelectric self-powered sensor for omnidirectional monitoring of wind speed and direction," *Nano Energy*, vol. 102, p. 107 717, 2022. DOI: 10.1016/j.nanoen.2022.107717.

[4] Y.-Y. Liu, Y.-X. Lv, and H.-B. Xue, "Intelligent wearable wrist pulse detection system based on piezoelectric sensor array," *Sensors*, vol. 23, no. 2, 2023, ISSN: 1424-8220. DOI: 10.3390/s23020835.

[5] H. Gutierrez *et al.*, "Fiber optic sensor arrays for real-time virtual instrumentation and control of flexible structures," in *Structural Health Monitoring, Damage Detection & Mechatronics, Volume 7*, Springer, 2016, pp. 9–22. DOI: 10.1007/978-3-319-29956-3_2.

[6] D. Son, S. Yim, and M. Sitti, "A 5-d localization method for a magnetically manipulated untethered robot using a 2-d array of hall-effect sensors," *IEEE/ASME transactions on mechatronics*, vol. 21, no. 2, pp. 708–716, 2015. DOI: 10.1109/TMECH.2015.2488361.

[7] N. Fischer, J. Kriechbaum, D. Berwanger, and F. Mathis-Ullrich, "Compliant hall-effect sensor array for passive magnetic instrument tracking," *IEEE Sensors Letters*, vol. 7, no. 3, pp. 1–4, 2023. DOI: 10.1109/LSENS.2023.3250971.

[8] I. Yoon *et al.*, "A capacitive micromachined ultrasonic transducer-based resonant sensor array for portable volatile organic compound detection with wireless systems," *Sensors*, vol. 19, no. 6, p. 1401, 2019. DOI: 10.3390/s19061401.

[9] C. Medrano-Sanchez, R. Igual-Catalan, V. H. Rodriguez-Ontiveros, and I. Plaza-Garcia, "Circuit Analysis of Matrix-Like Resistor Networks for Eliminating Crosstalk in Pressure Sensitive Mats," *IEEE Sensors Journal*, vol. 19, no. 18, pp. 8027–8036, 2019. DOI: 10.1109/JSEN.2019.2918592.

[10] X. Kong *et al.*, "Sensing distortion-induced fatigue cracks in steel bridges with capacitive skin sensor arrays," *Smart Materials and Structures*, vol. 27, no. 11, p. 115 008, 2018. DOI: 10.1088/1361-665X/aadbfb.

[11] Z. Ren, K. Cui, and Y. Sun, "Pipeline anti-vandalism monitoring system based on time division multiplexing interferometric fiber optic sensor array," *Optical Fiber Technology*, vol. 62, p. 102 470, 2021. DOI: 10.1016/j.yofte.2021.102470.

[12] T. Fu, Y. Wang, L. Qiu, and X. Tian, "Sector piezoelectric sensor array transmitter beamforming music algorithm based structure damage imaging method," *Sensors*, vol. 20, no. 5, p. 1265, 2020. DOI: 10.3390/s20051265.

[13] B. Ibrahim and R. Jafari, "Cuffless blood pressure monitoring from a wristband with calibration-free algorithms for sensing location based on bio-impedance sensor array and autoencoder," *Scientific reports*, vol. 12, no. 1, pp. 1–14, 2022. DOI: 10.1038/s41598-021-03612-1.

[14] Y. Sun and F. Gu, "Compressive sensing of piezoelectric sensor response signal for phased array structural health monitoring," *International Journal of Sensor Networks*, vol. 23, no. 4, pp. 258–264, 2017. DOI: 10.1504/IJSNET.2017.083531.

[15] L. Si and Q. Wang, "Rapid multi-damage identification for health monitoring of laminated composites using piezoelectric wafer sensor arrays," *Sensors*, vol. 16, no. 5, p. 638, 2016. DOI: 10.3390/s16050638.

[16] Z. Zhang *et al.*, "Oil-paper insulation partial discharge ultrasonic multifrequency sensing array based on fibre-optic fabry–perot sensor," *High Voltage*, vol. 7, no. 2, pp. 325–335, 2022. DOI: 10.1049/hve2.12123.

[17] Y. Yang *et al.*, "Evaluation of the transverse crack depth of rail bottoms based on the ultrasonic guided waves of piezoelectric sensor arrays," *Sensors*, vol. 22, no. 18, p. 7023, 2022. DOI: 10.3390/s22187023.

[18] I. M. da Fonseca, D. A. Rade, L. C. Goes, and T. de Paula Sales, "Attitude and vibration control of a satellite containing flexible solar arrays by using reaction wheels, and piezoelectric transducers as sensors and actuators," *Acta Astronautica*, vol. 139, pp. 357–366, 2017. DOI: 10.1016/j.actaastro.2017.07.018.

[19] H. Nhalil, M. Schultz, S. Amrusi, A. Grosz, and L. Klein, "Parallel array of planar hall effect sensors for high resolution magnetometry," *Journal of Applied Physics*, vol. 133, no. 20, p. 204 501, May 2023. DOI: 10.1063/5.0151569.

[20] Y. Ye, C. He, B. Liao, and G. Qian, "Capacitive proximity sensor array with a simple high sensitivity capacitance measuring circuit for human–computer interaction," *IEEE Sensors Journal*, vol. 18, no. 14, pp. 5906–5914, 2018. DOI: 10.1109/JSEN.2018.2840093.

[21] G. Geron, C. Prelle, H. Al Hajjar, J. Terrien, and M. U. Khan, "Characterization of a magnetic localization method based on hall effect sensor array for microrobot position tracking," *Journal of Micro-Bio Robotics*, pp. 1–13, 2023. DOI: 10.1007/s12213-023-00154-9.

[22] F. Piron, D. Morrison, M. R. Yuce, and J.-M. Redoute, "A review of single-photon avalanche diode time-of-flight imaging sensor arrays," *IEEE Sensors Journal*, vol. 21, no. 11, pp. 12 654–12 666, 2020. DOI: 10.1109/JSEN.2020.3039362.

[23] J.-O. Nilsson and I. Skog, "Inertial sensor arraysa literature review," in *2016 European Navigation Conference (ENC)*, IEEE, 2016, pp. 1–10. DOI: 10.1109/EURONAV.2016.7530551.

[24] M. Yang *et al.*, "Arrayed piezoresistive and inertial measurement unit sensor-integrated assistant training tennis racket for multipoint hand pressure monitoring and representative action recognition," *Science China Technological Sciences*, pp. 1–11, 2023. DOI: 10.1007/s11431-022-2377-7.

[25] W. Xia, P. Che, M. Ren, X. Zhang, and C. Cao, "A flexible p (vdf-trfe) piezoelectric sensor array for orientation identification of impulse stress," *Organic Electronics*, vol. 114, p. 106 729, 2023. DOI: 10.1016/j.orgel.2022.106729.

[26] J. H. Park *et al.*, "Feasibility study on fiber-optic inorganic scintillator array sensor system for muti-dimensional scanning of radioactive waste," *Nuclear Engineering and Technology*, vol. 55, no. 9, pp. 3206–3212, 2023. DOI: 10.1016/j.net.2023.06.002.

[27] A. D'Amico, G. Ferri, and A. Zompanti, "Sensor systems for breathprinting: A review of the current technologies for exhaled breath analysis based on a sensor array with the aim of integrating them in a standard and shared procedure," *Breath analysis*, pp. 49–79, 2019. DOI: 10.1016/B978-0-12-814562-3.00004-7.

[28] D. Li *et al.*, "Virtual sensor array based on piezoelectric cantilever resonator for identification of volatile organic compounds," *ACS Sensors*, vol. 7, no. 5, pp. 1555–1563, 2022. DOI: 10.1021/acssensors.2c00442.

[29] D. Esposito *et al.*, "A piezoresistive array armband with reduced number of sensors for hand gesture recognition," *Frontiers in neurorobotics*, vol. 13, p. 114, 2020. DOI: 10.3389/fnbot.2019.00114.

[30] M. Kim, H. Choi, K.-J. Cho, and S. Jo, "Single to multi: Data-driven high resolution calibration method for piezoresistive sensor array," *IEEE Robotics and Automation Letters*, vol. 6, no. 3, pp. 4970–4977, 2021. DOI: 10.1109/LRA.2021.3070823.

[31] J. Zhang *et al.*, "Design, fabrication, and implementation of an array-type mems piezoresistive intelligent pressure sensor system," *Micromachines*, vol. 9, no. 3, p. 104, 2018. DOI: 10.3390/mi9030104.

[32] A. K. M. Mahfuzul Islam *et al.*, "Programmable neuron array based on a 2-transistor multiplier using organic floating-gate for intelligent sensors," *IEEE Journal on Emerging and Selected Topics in Circuits and Systems*, vol. 7, no. 1, pp. 81–91, 2017. DOI: 10.1109/JETCAS.2016.2628411.

[33] B. Fang *et al.*, "A petal-array capacitive tactile sensor with micro-pin for robotic fingertip sensing," in *2020 3rd IEEE International Conference on Soft Robotics (RoboSoft)*, IEEE, 2020, pp. 452–457. DOI: 10.1109/RoboSoft48309.2020.9116047.

[34] F. Khatoon, M. Ravan, R. K. Amineh, and A. Byberi, "Hand gesture recognition pad using an array of inductive sensors," *IEEE Transactions on Instrumentation and Measurement*, vol. 72, pp. 1–11, 2023. DOI: 10.1109/TIM.2023.3280526.

[35] C. Tholin-Chittenden and M. Soleimani, "Planar array capacitive imaging sensor design optimization," *IEEE Sensors Journal*, vol. 17, no. 24, pp. 8059–8071, 2017. DOI: 10.1109/JSEN.2017.2719579.

[36] S. Dominguez-Gimeno, C. Medrano-Sanchez, R. Igual-Catalan, J. Martinez-Cesteros, and I. Plaza-Garcia, "An optimization approach to eliminate crosstalk in zero-potential circuits for reading resistive sensor arrays," *IEEE Sensors Journal*, vol. 23, no. 13, pp. 14 215–14 225, 2023. DOI: 10.1109/JSEN.2023.3277714.

[37] S. Guorong *et al.*, "Guided wave focusing imaging detection of pipelines by piezoelectric sensor array," *Journal of Sensors*, vol. 2022, no. 1, p. 4 731 341, DOI: 10.1155/2022/4731341.

[38] J. Chen, P. Liu, J. Hu, J. Yang, and C. Chen, "Design of an array of piezoresistive airflow sensors based on pressure loading mode for simultaneous detection of airflow velocity and direction," *Review of Scientific Instruments*, vol. 93, no. 2, p. 025 001, 2022. DOI: 10.1063/5.0073669.

[39] H. Liu *et al.*, "Active detection of small uxo-like targets through measuring electromagnetic responses with a magneto-inductive sensor array," *IEEE Sensors Journal*, vol. 21, no. 20, pp. 23 558–23 567, 2021. DOI: 10.1109/JSEN.2021.3107842.

Enhancing Urban Intersection Efficiency: Leveraging Visible Light Communication for Traffic Optimization

Manuel Augusto Vieira
Electronics Telecommunications and Computer Dept.
ISEL, CTS-UNINOVA and LASI
Lisbon, Portugal
email: mv@isel.ipl.pt

Manuela Vieira
Electronics Telecommunications and Computer Dept.
ISEL, CTS-UNINOVA ,LASI and NOVA School of Science and Technology
Lisbon, Portugal
email: mv@isel.ipl.pt

Gonçalo Galvão
Electronics Telecommunications and Computer Dept.
ISEL,
Lisbon, Portugal
email: A45903@alunos.isel.pt

Paula Louro
Electronics Telecommunications and Computer Dept.
ISEL, CTS-UNINOVA and LASI
Lisbon, Portugal
email: paula.louro@ isel.pt

Mário Véstias
Electronics Telecommunications and Computer Dept.
INESC INOV-Lab,
Lisboa, Portugal
email: mario.vestias@isel.pt

Abstract— **This paper presents a method using Visible Light Communication (VLC) to improve traffic signal efficiency and manage vehicle trajectories at urban intersections. It combines VLC localization services with learning-based traffic signal control for a multi-intersection traffic system. VLC enables communication between vehicles and infrastructure, aiding in joint transmission and data collection. The system aims to reduce waiting times for pedestrians and vehicles while enhancing safety. It's flexible, adapting to various traffic movements during signal phases. Cooperative mechanisms balance traffic flow between intersections, improving road network performance. Evaluated using the SUMO urban mobility simulator, it shows reduced waiting and travel times. An agent based scheme optimizes traffic signal scheduling based on VLC behaviors. The proposed approach is decentralized and scalable, suitable for real-world traffic scenarios.**

Keywords— Intelligent Transport System (ITS); Visible Light Communication; traffic signal control; urban intersections; traffic flow optimization; pedestrian safety; SUMO simulator; cooperative communication.

I. INTRODUCTION

The transportation landscape is rapidly evolving with the integration of smart sensors, Visible Light Communication (VLC), and artificial intelligence. VLC, using light intensity modulation from LEDs for data transmission, shows promise in revolutionizing Smart Mobility solutions and addressing societal goals such as reducing emissions and enhancing traffic safety [1]. It is widely implemented in various domains, including vehicular communication and traffic signal systems, highlighting its versatility and efficiency. However, current traffic signal optimization often overlooks pedestrian dynamics within intersections, necessitating comprehensive systems that consider both vehicular and pedestrian flows.

This paper proposes integrating VLC localization services with learning-based traffic signal control to manage pedestrian and vehicular traffic holistically [2]. Leveraging Reinforcement Learning (RL) concepts, the system optimizes traffic flow and enhances safety by considering interactions between vehicles and pedestrians. It introduces a pedestrian mobility model tailored for outdoor scenarios, analyzing multiple pedestrian behaviors, and incorporating them into the traffic signal control scheme. Validated through a case study in Lisbon's downtown, the model integrates pedestrian preferences to optimize routing algorithms [3].

Simulation experiments validate the effectiveness of the approach, utilizing real intersection data to demonstrate improved traffic flow and reduced waiting times.

The paper is structured to discuss, in Section 1, the importance of traffic control, in Section 2, the challenges it faces, and the motivation behind the proposed solution. It then delves, in Section 3, into the complexities of managing traffic in multi-intersection environments and, in Section 4, presents a model for traffic signal control incorporating machine learning elements, and analyzes simulated results. Finally, the conclusions, in Section 5, summarize the findings, insights gained, limitations, and potential future directions of the research.

II. TRAFFIC CONTROL CHALLENGES

A. *Pedestrian Dynamics and Complexity in Multi-Intersection Environments*

Traffic signal control research has traditionally prioritized vehicles, but there's now a shift towards pedestrian-friendly systems to prevent delays and accidents [4][5]. Sidewalks present challenges due to bi-directional flow, and differing speeds and movements between pedestrians and vehicles further complicate matters [6]. Our adaptive traffic control considers factors like queue lengths in neighboring intersections to balance scalability and efficiency. Our strategy is designed to address real-time traffic demands by modeling current and anticipated future traffic flows. Compared to traditional fixed coil detectors, our adaptive system in V2X environments gathers more granular data, including vehicle positions, speeds, queue lengths, and stopping times. V2V links play a crucial role in safety functionalities like pre-crash sensing, while V/P2I links provide valuable information to connected vehicles.

B. *Integrating V-VLC for Innovative Traffic Solutions*

With wireless tech advancements and Connected Vehicle (CV) [7] systems like V2V and V2I, integrating VLC localization with learning-based traffic control can manage both pedestrian and vehicular traffic in multi-intersections. It employs RL to enhance safety and reduce waiting times using V2V, V/P2I, and I2V/P communications. This approach synchronizes signal control in real-time, considering pedestrian and vehicle factors in the state and reward design, utilizing sidewalks for crucial pedestrian location info. SUMO simulations [8] assess the V-VLC system's effectiveness, with agent-based models learning to optimize traffic flow dynamically. Dynamic diagrams and state matrices illustrate the concept, showing potential for optimal traffic control policies.

III. UNLOCKING TRAFFIC CONTROL

A. *VLC background*

The V-VLC system, as depicted in Figure 1a, utilizes a mesh cellular hybrid structure with two controllers. The "mesh" controller at streetlights relays messages to vehicles, while the "mesh/cellular" hybrid controller acts as a border-router for edge computing [9][10].

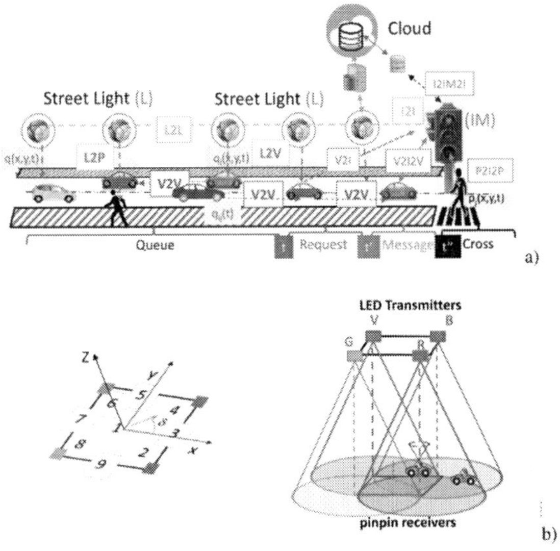

Figure 1. a) 2D representation of the simultaneous geo-localization as a function of node density, mobility and transmission range. b) Emitter and receivers' relative positions. Illustration of the coverage map in the unit cell: footprint regions (#1-#9) and steering angle codes (2-9).

The proposed architecture enables Infrastructure-to-Cloud communication (I2IM) through embedded computing platforms for processing and sensor interfacing. It also facilitates peer-to-peer communication (V2V) among vehicles, enhancing data sharing.

The Vehicular Visible Light Communication system (V-VLC) consists of a transmitter generating modulated light and a receiver detecting light variation, both wirelessly connected. LED-produced light is modulated using ON-OFF-keying (OOK) amplitude modulation (Figure 1b). Square unit cells in the environment feature tetra-chromatic white light (WLEDs) sources at cell corners. The V-VLC system uses coded signals transmitted by devices like streetlights, headlights, and traffic lights to communicate directly with identified vehicles and pedestrians (L/I2V/P), or indirectly between vehicles through their headlights (V2V). PIN-PIN photodetectors within mobile receivers receive and decode coded signals. This information aids in pinpointing positions within the network and provides directional guidance along cardinal points for drivers/pedestrians [10].

The system employs queue/request/response mechanisms and temporal/space relative pose concepts to manage vehicle passage through intersections. Vehicle speed is determined using transmitter IDs for tracking, while mesh nodes estimate indirect V2V relative poses in scenarios with multiple neighboring vehicles.

The integration of VLC enables direct monitoring among pedestrians, vehicles, and infrastructure, focusing on critical aspects such as queue formation and pedestrian corner density to enhance road safety. P2I2P communication enables travel time calculations, while real-time data on speed and waiting times are analyzed using transmitter tracking IDs.

B. *Traffic Scenario and Phasing Diagram*

The simulated scenario, as shown in Figure 2a, features two intersections, each with two 4-way junctions, consisting of 2 lanes per arm spanning 100 meters in total length.

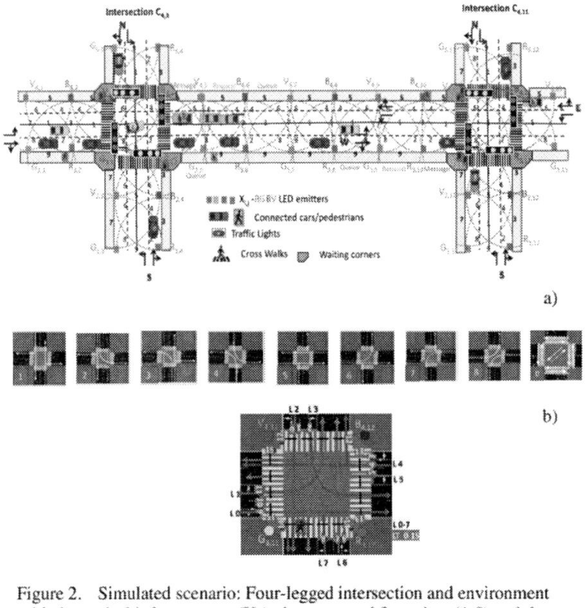

Figure 2. Simulated scenario: Four-legged intersection and environment with the optical infrastructure (X_{ij}), the generated footprints (1-9) and the connected cars and pedestrians. b) Phasing diagram and schematic diagram of the C2 intersection with coded lanes (L/0-7) and traffic lights (TL/0-15).

Traffic flows from compass directions, with lanes indicating movement options: right lanes for right turns or going straight, and left lanes for left turns only. Central traffic light systems, regulated by Intelligent Managers (IMs), control traffic. Features like emitters (streetlamps), pedestrian lanes, waiting areas, and crosswalks are integrated. Four traffic flows along cardinal points are considered, with road request and response segments offering binary choices (turn left/straight or turn right). Assumptions include a total influx of 2300 cars per hour, primarily from east and west directions, with 25% expected to turn and 75% to continue straight. Pedestrian influx is around 11200 per hour, crossing in all directions at an average speed of 3 km/h. Figure 2b outlines intersection phase progressions within a structured cycle length, comprising eight vehicular phases and an exclusive pedestrian phase. Each phase is subdivided into discrete time sequences, providing a comprehensive temporal framework [11][12].

Each flow (illustrated by the different vehicle colors) comprises vehicles moving straight or making left turns, with specific vehicles representing top requests in the sequence. The assumption is that specific vehicles, labeled a_1, b_1, a_2, b_2, a_3, c_1, b_3, e_1, a_4, c_2, a_5, and f_1, represent the top requests in the given sequence.

C. *Communication protocol, coding, and decoding techniques*

Data transmission in the VLC system follows a synchronous approach using a 64-bit data frame structure. Information is encoded using On-Off Keying (OOK) modulation, with each luminaire containing WLEDs (RGBV), enabling simultaneous transmission of four signals. A PIN-PIN demultiplexer decodes the message based on calibrated amplitudes of RGBV signals. The communication protocol includes components like Start of Frame (SoF) for synchronization, Identification Blocks encoding communication type (COM) and localization (position, time), and other ID Blocks for additional identifiers, Traffic Message containing vehicle information, and End of Frame (EoF) indicating the end of transmission. This structured protocol ensures efficient encoding and decoding of critical movement information, maintaining synchronization and data integrity in the VLC system. In Table 1, the communication protocol is depicted.

TABLE I. COMMUNICATION PROTOCOL.

		COM	Position		ID (veic)		Time				payload				
I2V	Sync	1	x	y	0 bits		END	Hour	Min	Sec					EOF
V2V	Sync	2	x	y	Lane (0-7)	Veic. (nr)	END	Hour	Min	Sec	Car IDx	Car IDy	nr behind		EOF
V2I	Sync	3	x	y	TL (0-15)	Veic. (nr).	END	Hour	Min	Sec	Car IDx	Car IDy	nr behind		EOF
I2V	Sync	4	x	y	TL (0-15)	ID Veic.	END	Hour	Min	Sec	Car IDx	Car IDy	nr behind		EOF
P2I	Sync	5	x	y	TL (0-15)	Direct.	END	Hour	Min	Sec					EOF
I2P	Sync	6	x	y	TL (0-15)	Phase	END	Hour	Min	Sec					EOF

Decoding the information received from the photocurrent signal captured by the photodetector involves a critical step reliant on a pre-established calibration curve [12]. This curve meticulously maps each conceivable decoding level to a sequence of bits. Essentially, the calibration curve serves as a guide, facilitating the establishment of associations between photocurrent thresholds and specific bit sequences.

IV. RESULTS

A. *VLC Algorithms*

Figure 3, displays the decoded optical signals (at the top of the figures) and the signals received (MUX) by the receivers in a V2V (COM 2) and V2I (COM 3) communication scenario involving a leader vehicle a_o at position ($R_{3,10}$, $G_{3,11}$, $B_{4,10,}$). This vehicle is communicating with the agent at the second intersection (C2) on lane L0 (direction E) at 10:25:46 and is followed by three other vehicles (Veic. nr) V_1, V_2, and V_3 with the same direction, located at positions (IDx,y) $R_{3,8}$, $G_{3,6}$ and $R_{3,4}$, respectively.

Figure 4 demonstrates the MUX signal and the decoded messages sent by the traffic lights to pedestrians ($I2P_{1,2}$). This visual representation helps to understand the communication between pedestrians waiting in the corners and the corresponding traffic lights, providing insights into the signals exchanged for pedestrian crossings at both intersections (C1 and C2).

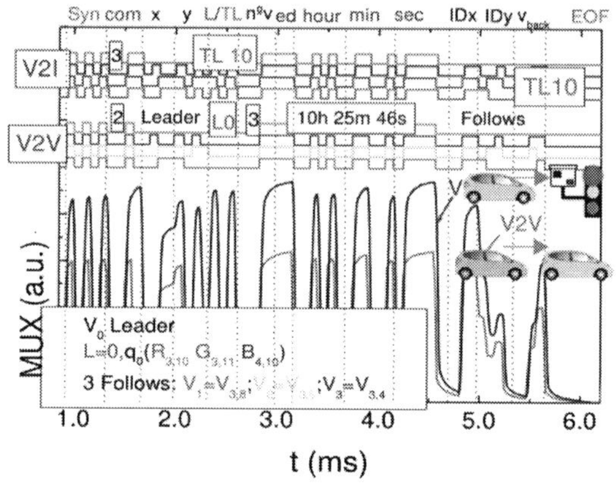

Figure 3. MUX signal request assigned to different types of communication. On the top the decoded messages are displayed.

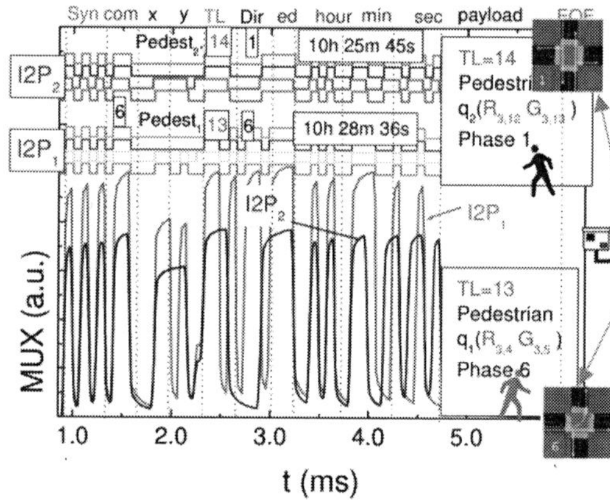

Figure 4. Normalized MUX signal responses and the corresponding decoded messages, displayed at the top, sent by the IM to pedestrians waiting in the corners ($I2P_{1,2}$) (b) at various frame times.

Upon pedestrian q_2 receiving information from the traffic light C2, it becomes evident that the current active phase is N-S (Phase 1), signifying that the pedestrian did not arrive in time for their designated phase (Phase 0). Consequently, the pedestrian is required to wait for an estimated cycle time of 3 (cycle time) minutes before being granted the opportunity to cross. Subsequently, the pedestrian crosses the crosswalk, covering the distance to the next intersection in approximately 1 minute and 50 seconds. Upon arrival, the pedestrian waits in the designated waiting zone at position $R_{3,4}$-$G_{3,5}$ until the pedestrian phase becomes active once again. At 10:28:35, the pedestrian establishes communication with traffic light TL13 at the C1 ($P_1$2I). The traffic light promptly responds ($I2P_1$) at 10:28:36, providing crucial information that the currently active phase is the final one in the cycle (Phase 6). These interactions highlight the effectiveness of the pedestrian's communication with the traffic lights, enabling them to stay informed about the active phase, waiting time, and make decisions accordingly.

B. Dynamic Traffic Control: Integrating Pedestrian Consideration

Assessing the effectiveness of the proposed V-VLC system in multi-intersection utilizes the Simulation of Urban MObility (SUMO), employing agent-based simulations. SUMO tests traffic control algorithms, manages intersections, and oversees pedestrian crossings, mirroring real-world conditions. For data analysis, SUMO collects and analyzes simulation data, including vehicle trajectories, travel times, congestion levels, and pedestrian movements.

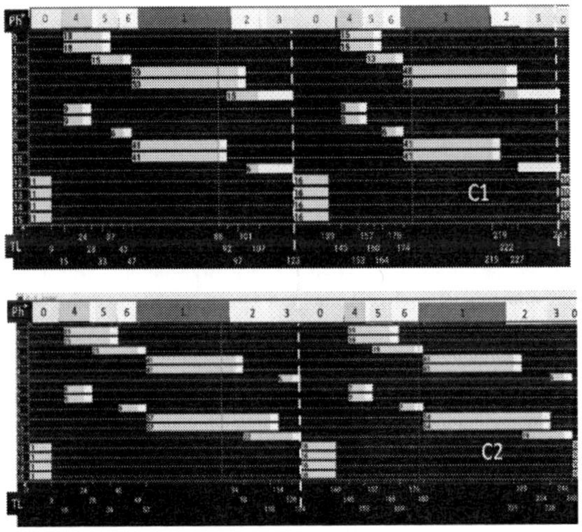

Figure 5. State phasing diagrams for C1 and C2 intersections.

The simulation scenario, adapted to the SUMO simulator, provides insights into traffic light signals and vehicle/pedestrian movements within the terminals. In Figure 5 a state diagram was generated for C2 intersection, incorporating both vehicles in the lanes (2300v/h) and pedestrians (11200 p/h) in the sidewalks during two cycles of 120 seconds. These diagrams offer insights into the dynamic behavior of traffic light signals and carrier/pedestrian movements within the simulated terminals. As can be observed in the diagrams it is possible to distinguish the different cycles that occur during the simulation. It always begins with a pedestrian phase (Phase 0), during which some pedestrians can cross the crosswalk, turning red for pedestrians starting from 11 seconds. Then, phases dedicated to vehicles (Phases 1-8) take place until it concludes at 123 seconds. At this moment, the second cycle begins, with the pedestrian phase becoming active again. The same process repeats until 247 seconds, marking the end of this second cycle and the initiation of a third cycle. These diagrams align with the analysis conducted for pedestrians.

V. INTELLIGENT TRAFFIC CONTROL SYSTEM

With the data collected on vehicles via VLC through the cells in Figure 1, implemented via lamps along the roads as shown in Figure 2, an intelligent traffic system must be developed to optimize traffic flow at intersections. This system utilizes Reinforcement Learning (RL), a machine learning paradigm where an agent learns to make decisions by interacting with its environment. Agents in RL aim to achieve a goal in uncertain, potentially complex environments by receiving feedback in the form of rewards or punishments. The fundamental idea is for the agent to learn optimal behavior or strategies through trial and error.

At each time step t, the agent receives a state input s_t, based on the observation of the environment and then executes an action a_t, that transforms the state observed to a next state s_{t+1}. Then the reward r_t, a metric that defines how good the action was for the environment, is calculated. In this case, the reward is defined by (1), using the accumulated total waiting time, atw_t, as a metric for vehicles (*veh*) and pedestrians (*ped*). $atwt_t$ and $atwt_{t-1}$ are the accumulated total waiting time of all the cars/pedestrians in the intersection captured respectively at agentstep t and agentstep $t-1$. The weights of the p_{veh} and p_{ped} are set based on the desired priority that the agent should have towards vehicles and pedestrians during network training. The agent will learn a policy that benefits one more than the other, or keeps the system balanced if the weights are equal.

If the agent's behavior leads to positive environmental reward, which indicates that the waiting time is longer in the past, *t-1*, than at the present moment, *t*, then the tendency of producing this behavior by the agent will be strengthened, and vice versa. The goal is to maximize the cumulative discounted reward.

$$r_t = p_{veh}(atwt_{veh,t-1} - atwt_{veh,t}) + p_{ped}(atwt_{ped,t-1} - atwt_{ped,t}) \quad (1)$$

This experience $e_x = (s_t, a_t, r_t, s_{t+1})$ will be stored in the replay memory, to be used in the future to train the agent. The replay memory is a dataset of an agent's experiences $D_t = (e_1, e_2, \dots, e_t)$, which are gathered when the agent interact with the environment as time goes by (t = 1, 2..., n).

To train the agent, the deep Q-Learning technique is employed, leveraging the Q-Learning algorithm [11][13]. The Q-value represents the expected cumulative reward of taking a particular action in a particular state and following the optimal policy thereafter. These Q-values are predicted by a Neural Network (NN) that takes the state as input and outputs Q-values for each possible action.

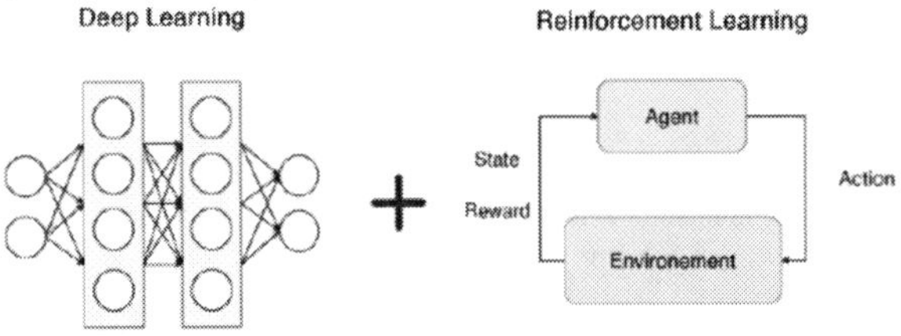

Figure 6. Deep Reinforcement Learning.

The Q-value represents the expected cumulative reward of taking a specific action in each state while following the optimal policy thereafter.

A Neural Network (NN) predicts these Q-values by taking the state as input and outputting Q-values for each possible action. The state of the environment comprises 100 cells at each intersection, indicating the presence of vehicles or pedestrians. These cells are set to '1' if occupied and '0' if not. Each lane, divided into 10 cells, indicates vehicle movement toward the intersection, with cell sizes increasing farther from the intersection. With 8 lanes per junction, there are 80 vehicle cells per intersection. For pedestrians, only the waiting zones are considered, each divided into 5 cells, totaling 20 pedestrian cells per intersection, as drafted in Figure 6.

The neural network's input layer consists of 100 neurons representing the state of the environment. This is followed by five hidden layers, each with 400 neurons using Rectified

Linear Units (ReLUs). The output layer features nine neurons, each representing the Q-values for potential actions. To refine Q-value predictions, a Mean Squared Error (MSE) function quantifies the disparity between predicted and target Q-values, enhancing the learning process. N represents the number of samples stored in memory, and Q_{target} and Q_{pred} denote the target and predicted values, respectively. After each training episode, target Q-values for action-state pairs are calculated based on (2).

$$MSE_{Loos} = \frac{1}{N}\sum_{i=1}^{N}\left(Q_{target} - Q_{pred}\right)^2 \quad (2)$$

N is the number of samples stored in memory, and the target and predicted value, Q_{target} and Q_{pred}, respectively. After each episode of training, the target Q-values for action-state pairs are calculated based on (3).

$$Q_{target} = r_t + \gamma.\, maxQ_{pred}(s_{t+1}, a') \quad (3)$$

The nine Q-values at the neural network's output correspond to the nine actions shown in Figure 7. The agent selects the action that best suits the current traffic situation, without following a predefined order. Conversely, today's dynamic traffic systems at junctions follow a fixed sequence of phases, as shown in Figure 7.

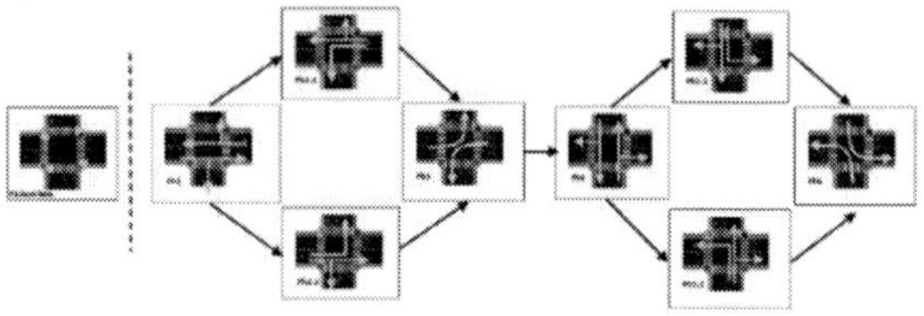

Figure 7. Nine possible actions that can be chosen by the agent.

This can result in activating a phase that does not align with current traffic needs. The next section compares these two systems to highlight their differences and evaluate their effectiveness.

VI. SIMULATION RESULTS

A. *Training Results*

To evaluate the behaviour of the intelligent traffic control system in relation to pedestrian and vehicle scenarios, a comparison was made with the dynamic traffic control system. The neural network used was trained with a reward system that weighted the waiting times for vehicles (p_{veh}) and pedestrians (p_{ped}) equally, for 300 epochs, each lasting one hour. Both systems considered the same generation rates for pedestrians and vehicles, totalling 2300 vehicles and 11000 pedestrians in the traffic scenario.8

Figure 8 shows the cumulative negative reward from training the network for both agents. Both agents evolved and learned from their traffic experiences throughout the episodes. The curves converged towards less negative reward values, indicating better decision-making over time.

In Figure 9a, which represents the high vehicle and pedestrian scenario, the intelligent system significantly outperforms the dynamic system. The dynamic system peaks at around 1500 waiting pedestrians in the first 25 minutes, while the intelligent system peaks at just 400 pedestrians. Figure 9b shows a smaller difference in the high vehicle and low pedestrian scenario, where the dynamic system peaks at 275 pedestrians in the first 15 minutes, compared to 150 for the intelligent system. This disparity arises because the intelligent system adapts phases dynamically to current traffic conditions, unlike the dynamic system, which follows a fixed cycle. The pedestrian phase in the dynamic system, appearing every 120 seconds, results in periodic peaks in waiting pedestrians.

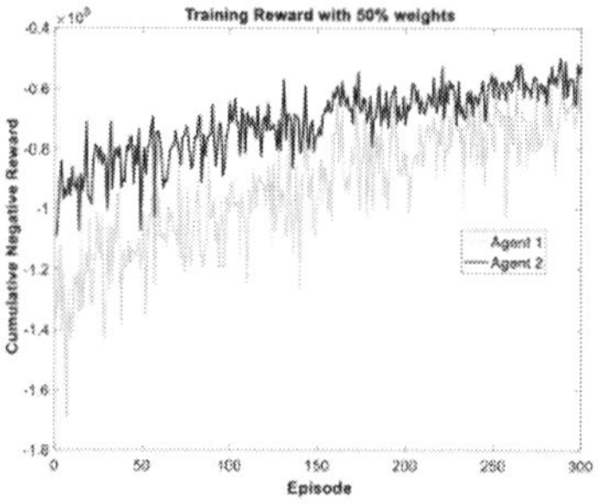

Figure 8. Cumulative Negative reward for both agents in training.

After training the network, tests were conducted to compare both systems under two traffic scenarios representing peak hour conditions. The first scenario involved high vehicle and pedestrian traffic (High-High) with 2300 cars and 11000 pedestrians. The second scenario had high vehicle traffic but low pedestrian traffic (High-Low), with 2300 cars and 5600 pedestrians.

B. *Testing results – High-High and High-Low scenarios*

Figures 9a and 9b display the number of pedestrians waiting in zones at the two junctions for both traffic scenarios.

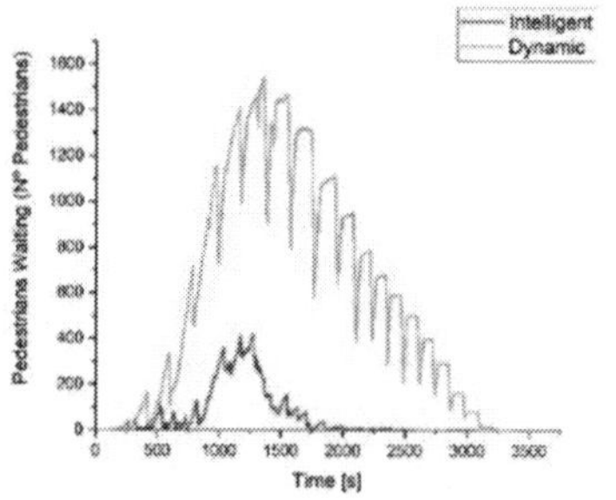

a)

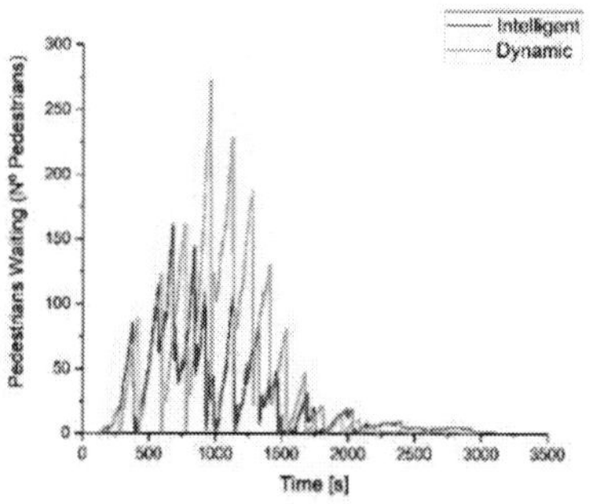

b)

Figure 9. Comparison of the number of pedestrians stopped waiting in both systems for the High-High (a) and High-Low (b) scenarios.

Figures 10a and 10b illustrate vehicle waiting times under both scenarios. Figure 10a shows that the intelligent system reaches a peak of waiting vehicles between 8 and 15 minutes due to higher pedestrian traffic affecting vehicle flow. In contrast, Figure 10b indicates a peak at around 15 minutes when pedestrian traffic is lower, allowing the system to balance vehicle and pedestrian phases better.

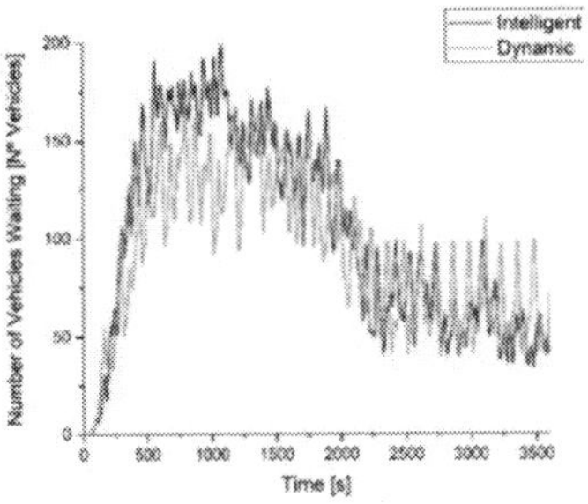

a)

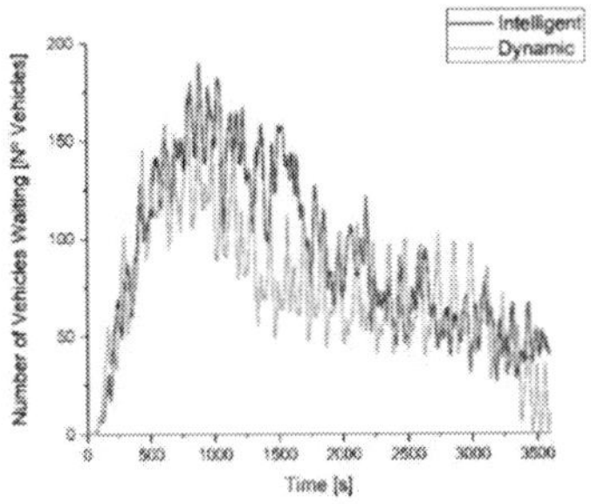

b)

Figure 10. Comparison of the number of cars in the entire environment for both systems for the High-High (a) and High-Low (b) scenarios.

Despite both scenarios having high vehicle traffic, the intelligent system manages fewer waiting vehicles in the low pedestrian scenario. The dynamic system shows consistent behavior with a 120-second cycle time, but the high pedestrian count negatively impacts vehicle dispatch, suggesting that many waiting pedestrians might lead to poor vehicle flow.

VII. CONCLUSIONS

This paper sets the groundwork for advancing intelligent traffic management by highlighting the potential of VLC technology to enhance safety and efficiency at urban intersections. Our focus was on optimizing both vehicular and pedestrian traffic, addressing the previously overlooked aspect of pedestrian phases. By analyzing agents' behavior and decision-making, particularly concerning pedestrian safety, we aimed to refine the timing of pedestrian phases.

In the domain of traffic optimization, our state representation incorporates environmental information, vehicle and pedestrian distribution data from V-VLC messages, and a proposed phasing diagram guiding agent actions. We developed dynamic and intelligent control system models to securely manage traffic at two connected intersections. Through Reinforcement Learning and the SUMO simulator, we conducted a thorough analysis. With an agent at each intersection, the system optimizes traffic lights based on communication from VLC-ready vehicles, devising strategies to enhance flow and coordinate with other agents for overall traffic optimization.

Overall, the intelligent system demonstrates superior adaptability and efficiency. It manages to reduce pedestrian waiting times while still maintaining a reasonable level of vehicle flow. In comparison, the dynamic system's fixed cycle often leads to longer pedestrian wait times, which can cause significant congestion. Therefore, the intelligent system proves to be more effective in handling the traffic scenarios studied, providing a better balance between vehicle and pedestrian needs.

ACKNOWLEDGMENT

This work was sponsored by FCT – Fundação para a Ciência e a Tecnologia, within the Research Unit CTS – Center of Technology and Systems, reference UIDB/00066/2020 and by IPL project reference IPL/IDI&CA2024/NUTRAMISEL.

REFERENCES

[1] D. O'Brien et al., "Indoor Visible Light Communications: challenges and prospects," Proc. SPIE 7091, 709106, pp. 60-68, 2008.

[2] X. Liang, X. Du, G. Wang, and Z. Han, "A Deep Reinforcement Learning Network for Traffic Light Cycle Control," in IEEE Transactions on Vehicular Technology, vol. 68, no. 2, pp. 1243-1253, Feb. 2019, doi: 10.1109/TVT.2018.2890726.

[3] I. Sousa, P. Queluz, A. Rodrigues, and P. Vieira, "Realistic mobility modeling of pedestrian traffic in wireless networks". In 2011 IEEE EUROCON-International Conference on Computer as a Tool, pp. 1-4, IEEE , 2011.

[4] T. Ding, S. Wang, J. Xi, L. Zheng, and Q. Wang, "Psychology-Based Research on Unsafe Behavior by Pedestrians When Crossing the Street". Adv. Mech. Eng., 7, 203867, pp. 1-6, 2015.

[5] J. Oskarbski, L. Guminska, M. Miszewski, and I. Oskarbska,. "Analysis of Signalized Intersections" in the Context of Pedestrian Traffic. Transportation Research Procedia, 14, pp. 2138-2147, 2016, doi:10.1016/j.trpro.2016.05.229

[6] Y. Elbaum, A. Novoselsky, and E. A. Kagan, "Queueing Model forTraffic Flow Control in the Road Intersection," Mathematics, 10, 3997, 2022. doi: 10.3390/math10213997.

[7] S. Yousefi, E. Altman, R. El-Azouzi, and M. Fathy, "Analytical Model for Connectivity in Vehicular Ad Hoc Networks," IEEE Transactions on Vehicular Technology, 57, pp. 3341-3356, 2008.

[8] Alvarez Lopez et al., "Microscopic Traffic Simulation using SUMO. In: 2019 IEEE Intelligent Transportation Systems Conference (ITSC), pp. 2575-2582. IEEE. The 21st IEEE International Conference on Intelligent Transportation Systems, , Maui, USA, pp. 4.-7, Nov. 2018.

[9] A. Yousefpour et al., "All one needs to know about fog computing and related edge computing paradigms: A complete survey", Journal of Systems Architecture, vol. 98, pp. 289-330, 2019.

[10] M. A. Vieira, M. Vieira, P. Louro, and P. Vieira, "Cooperative vehicular visible light communication in smarter split intersections," Proc. SPIE 12139, Optical Sensing and Detection VII, 1213905, 17 May 2022; doi: 10.1117/12.2621069.

[11] M. A. Vieira, G. Galvão, M. Vieira, M. Véstias, P. Vieira, and P. Louro, "Traffic Signaling and Cooperative Trajectories based on Visible Light Communication," Sensors and Electronic Instrumentation Advances, pp. 23, 2023.

[12] M. A. Vieira, G. Galvão, M. Vieira, P. Louro, M. Vestias, and P. Vieira, "Enhancing Urban Intersection Efficiency: Visible Light Communication and Learning-Based Control for Traffic Signal Optimization and Vehicle Management". Symmetry 2024, 16, 240. https://doi.org/10.3390/ sym16020240.

[13] G. Galvão et al., "Traffic signals and cooperative trajectories at urban intersections: leveraging visible light communication for implementation," Proc. SPIE 12906, Light-Emitting Devices, Materials, and Applications XXVIII, 1290600 (13 March 2024); doi : 10.1117/12.3000529.

Indoor Guidance in Multi-Terminal Airports through Visible Light Communication

Manuela Vieira
Electronics Telecommunications and Computer Dept.
ISEL, CTS-UNINOVA, LASI and NOVA School of Science and Technology
Lisbon, Portugal
email: mv@isel.ipl.pt

Manuel Augusto Vieira
Electronics Telecommunications and Computer Dept.
ISEL, CTS-UNINOVA and LASI
Lisbon, Portugal
email: mv@ isel.pt

Gonçalo Galvão
Electronics Telecommunications and Computer Dept.
ISEL
Lisbon, Portugal
email: A45903@alunos.isel.pt

Paula Louro
Electronics Telecommunications and Computer Dept.
ISEL, CTS-UNINOVA and LASI
Lisbon, Portugal
email: paula.louro@ isel.pt

Alessandro Fantoni
Electronics Telecommunications and Computer Dept.
ISEL, CTS-UNINOVA and LASI
Lisbon, Portugal
email: alessandro.fantoni@ isel.pt

***Abstract*— This study introduces an innovative method for guiding navigation in busy airports using Visible Light Communication (VLC) technology. By utilizing existing lighting fixtures to transmit encoded messages via light signals, users can receive location-specific guidance. The system employs tetrachromatic Light Emitting Diodes (LEDs) and VLC capabilities to efficiently transmit data, supported by a mesh cellular hybrid structure that enhances flexibility without the need for traditional gateways. Integrating VLC into Edge/Fog architecture maximizes its benefits, such as wireless connectivity and secure communication while leveraging existing infrastructure. This integration allows for distributed data processing, storage, and communication at the network edge, improving system performance. The study develops a detailed airport model and analyzes navigation for pedestrians and luggage/passenger carriers. Users equipped with PINPIN optical sensors interpret light signals for localization and positioning, supported by a tailored communication protocol and coding techniques for reliable transmission.**

Keywords-Visible Light Communication (VLC); Wayfinding; Indoor Navigation; User Behavior; Agent-Based simulator; Edge/Fog Architecture.

I. INTRODUCTION

VLC is a data transmission technology [1]-[3] that can easily be employed in indoor environments since it can use the existing LED lighting infrastructure with simple modifications [4]-[6]. In the sequence, we propose to use modulated visible light, carried out by white low-cost LEDs. LEDs are capable of switching to different light intensity levels at a very fast rate, imperceptible to the human eye. This functionality can be used for communication where the data is encoded in the emitting light. A mobile receiver is used to demodulate and decode the electrical signal generated at a photodetector. This means that the LEDs are twofold by providing illumination as well as communication. Multicolored LEDs based luminaires can provide further possibilities for signal modulation and detection in VLC systems [7]. The use of white polychromatic LEDs offers the possibility of Wavelength Division Multiplexing (WDM) which enhances the transmission data rate. A WDM receiver based on tandem a-SiC:H/a-Si:H PIN/PIN light-controlled filter was used [8][9]. Here, when different visible signals are encoded in the same optical transmission path, the device multiplexes the different optical channels, performs different filtering processes (amplification, switching, and wavelength conversion) and finally decodes the encoded signals recovering the transmitted information.

Fine-grained indoor localization technology presents various applications, particularly beneficial in complex environments like airports. By implementing VLC technology, the indoor navigation can be significantly improved, offering users precise location information and enhancing their overall experience in crowded indoor environments [10][11]. Passengers can receive precise directions to boarding gates, check-in counters, baggage claim areas, lounges, and other amenities, reducing confusion and enhancing their overall experience. Additionally, it enables real-time tracking and management of assets such as luggage carts and maintenance equipment, optimizing their deployment and utilization throughout the airport. For airport retailers, indoor localization facilitates personalized promotions, wayfinding assistance, and location-based services, leading to increased sales and customer satisfaction. Ultimately, this technology streamlines operations, improves passenger experience, and enhances safety and security measures, contributing to a more efficient and enjoyable air travel experience for all stakeholders.

This paper is organized as follows: In the Introduction, the challenges faced in navigating multi-terminal airports are presented, the existing literature is reviewed, and the concept of utilizing VLC for indoor navigation is justified. Section 2 describes the approach used for supporting wayfinding activities in multi-terminal airports using VLC technology. In Section 3, the methodology for generating the airport model is presented, and the analysis of two types of users (pedestrians and luggage/passenger carriers) is described. Section 4 describes the agent-based simulator used to control traffic for both user categories and presents and discusses the results on users halting and average speeds and different geometric scenarios. Finally, in Section 5, the conclusions summarize the key findings of the study and suggest future research directions to further enhance indoor navigation systems using VLC technology.

II. METHODOLOGY

A. VLC background

The system model is structured around two primary modules: the transmitter and the receiver (Figure 1).

The transmitter module plays a crucial role in converting sender data into byte format before transmitting it as light signals. White light tetra-chromatic sources (WLEDs) with four polychromatic LEDs are utilized, each representing a data channel. Each luminaire is composed of four polychromatic WLEDs framed at the corners of a square. The setup, shown in Figure 1a. At each node, only one chip is modulated for data transmission (Figure 1a), the Red (R: 626 nm, 25 $\mu W/cm^2$), the Green (G: 530 nm, 46 $\mu W/cm^2$), the Blue (B: 470 nm, 60 $\mu W/cm^2$) or the Violet (V, 400 nm, 150 $\mu W/cm^2$) and the intensities of the other is controlled to give the white light perception.

The ON-OFF Keying (OOK) modulation scheme is used, where light presence signifies a binary "1" and absence a binary "0." The signal is transmitted through the optical channel and received by a VLC receiver, which extracts the data using a MUX photodetector acting as an active filter. The integrated filter consists of a p-i'(a-SiCH)-n/p-i(a-Si:H)-n amorphous heterostructure with low conductivity doped layers as displayed in Figure 1b. It transforms the light signal into an electrical signal that is subsequently decoded to extract the transmitted information. The obtained voltage is then processed, by using signal conditioning techniques (adaptive bandpass filtering and amplification, triggering, and demultiplexing), until the data signal is reconstructed at the data processing unit (digital conversion, decoding, and decision) [12].

The receiver needs to be positioned to overlap the range circles of multiple transmitters, resulting in a multiplexed (MUX) signal for both positioning and data transmission. The grid sizes prevent overlapping from adjacent grid points, defining nine fingerprint regions per unit square cell. The device computes the centroid of received coordinates, establishing it as the reference point position, offering nuanced resolution in localizing the mobile device within each cell.

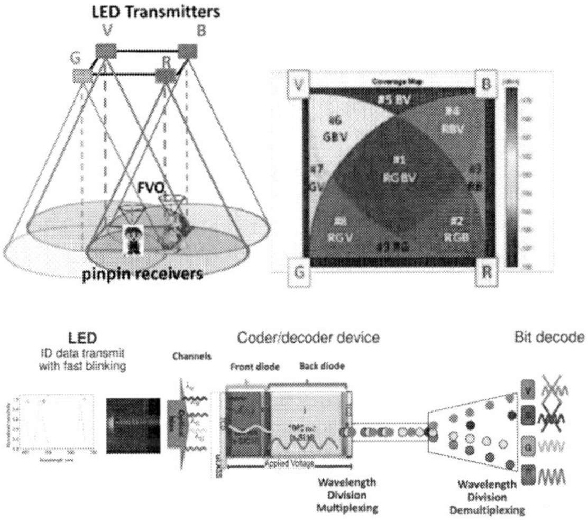

a)

b)

Figure 1. a) Transmitters and receivers 3D relative positions, footprints and coverage map in the square topology. b) Configuration and operation of the PINPIN receiver.

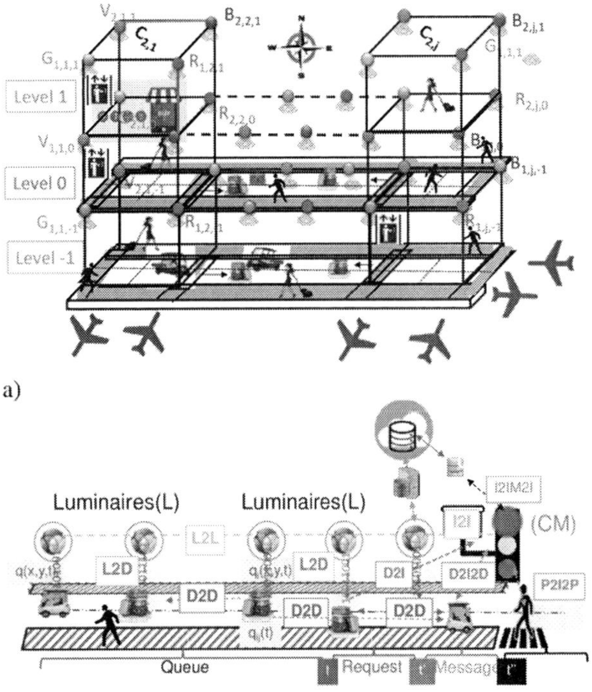

a)

b)

Figure 2. a) lighting plan. b) One lane draft of the Edge/Frog hybrid architecture.

B. *Lighting Plan Layout, Architecture and Geolocation*

Building a geometry model of buildings' interiors is complex. Indoor VLC cell design is especially important since, being man-made; buildings, such as these commonly follow basic shapes. A square lattice topology for the luminaires was considered for each level, as illustrated in Figure 2a.

This topology is represented using the *x*, *y*, and *z* axes to simplify both the figure comprehension and the distance between any pair of nodes. Each room/crossing/exit represents a node, and a path is the link between nodes. Figure 2a the 3D building model is draft. The user positions can be represented as $q\ (x,\ y,\ z,\ t)$ by providing the horizontal positions $(x,\ y)$ and the correct floor number *z*. The ground floor is level 0 and the user can go both below (z<0) and above (z>0) from there. In this study, the 3D model generation is based on footprints of a multi-level building that are collected from available sources (luminaires) and are displayed on the user receiver for user orientation. It is a requirement that the destination can be targeted by user request to the CM and that floor changes are notified. Each unit cell can be identified as $C_{i,j,k}$ where i, j, k are the x, y, z position in the square unit cell of the top left node.

In VLC tracking, geographical coordinates are used to guide users through buildings and towards specific destinations. This is facilitated by employing cells for positioning and a Central Manager (CM) to manage the system and generate optimal routes. A mesh cellular hybrid structure is introduced to enhance network architecture, enabling direct device-to-device communication and secure pathways. Each WLED emits a unique VLC signal, serving as an identification beacon, allowing precise user trajectory determination. The indoor route, containing spatial and temporal data, provides valuable insights into user movements. Users personalize their points of interest for wayfinding services, and average speeds are assigned based on the device type. Information is transmitted to the appropriate receivers by emitters within the infrastructure, such as Light Traffic controllers or signboards, positioned at crosswalks. In Figure 2b, the edge/fog architecture and the request communications between the Devices (D2D), the Devices and the Infrastructures (D2I) or the responses from the Infrastructure to the Devices /pedestrians (I2D/P) is draft. The user positions can be represented as q (x, y, z, t) by providing the horizontal positions $(x,\ y)$ [13].

C. *Communication protocol, coding, and decoding techniques*

Data transmission in the VLC system follows a synchronous approach using a 64-bit data frame structure. Information is encoded using OOK modulation, with each luminaire containing WLEDs (RGBV), enabling simultaneous transmission of four signals. A PIN-PIN demultiplexer decodes the message based on calibrated amplitudes of RGBV signals. The communication protocol includes components like Start of Frame (SoF) for synchronization, Identification Blocks encoding communication type (COM) and localization (position, time), and other ID Blocks for additional identifiers, Traffic Message containing vehicle information, and End of Frame (EoF) indicating the end of transmission. This structured protocol ensures efficient encoding and decoding of critical movement information, maintaining synchronization and data integrity in the VLC system. In Table 1, the communication protocol is depicted. Decoding the information received from the photocurrent signal captured by the photodetector involves a critical step reliant on a pre-established calibration curve [14].

TABLE I. COMMUNICATION PROTOCOL.

	SoF	COM	Position		ID (device)		Time				payload				EoF
I2D	Sync	1	x	y	0 bits		END	Hour	Min	Sec					EOF
D2D	Sync	2	x	y	Lane (0-7)	Device. (nr)	END	Hour	Min	Sec	Device IDx	DeviceI Dy	nr behind		EOF
D2I	Sync	3	x	y	TL (0-15)	Device (nr).	END	Hour	Min	Sec	Device IDx	DeviceI Dy	nr behind		EOF
I2D	Sync	4	x	y	TL (0-15)	ID Device	END	Hour	Min	Sec	Device IDx	DeviceI Dy	nr behind		EOF
P2I	Sync	5	x	y	TL (0-15)	N,S, E,W	END	Hour	Min	Sec					EOF
I2P	Sync	6	x	y	TL (0-15)	Phase	END	Hour	Min	Sec					EOF

This curve meticulously maps each conceivable decoding level to a sequence of bits. Essentially, the calibration curve serves as a guide, facilitating the establishment of associations between photocurrent thresholds and specific bit sequences.

III. AIRPORT MODEL

The capacity of an airport is closely tied to its gateways, boarding areas, and aircraft door layouts. Assigning these areas involves a coordinated process, tailored to specific objectives and criteria for each scenario. Objectives may include enhancing customer service by minimizing travel distances for pedestrians or passenger/luggage carriers during landing, transit, baggage claim, terminal changes, or shopping.

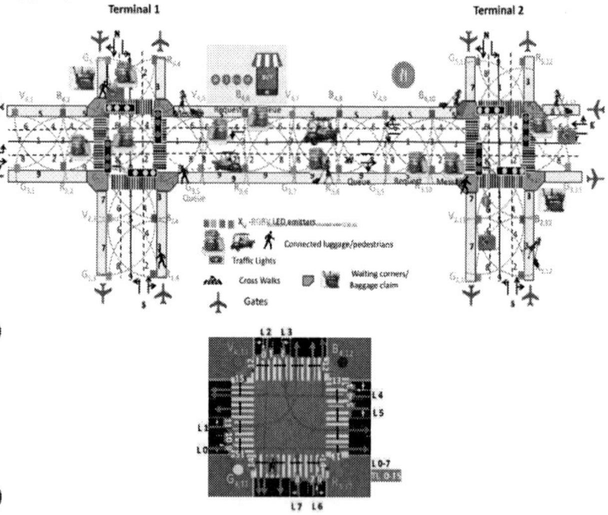

a)

b)

Figure 3. a) Simulated scenario and environment with the optical infrastructure (Xij), the generated footprints (1-9) and the connected luggage and pedestrians' flow. b) Schematic diagram of Terminal 2 with coded lanes (L/0-7) and traffic lights (TL/0-15)

Airports are assessed based on factors like walking distances between terminal facilities and accessibility to ground transportation and parking. This research enhances our understanding of pedestrian behavior within terminal corridors, informing better decisions in terminal facility design. The airport model is generated using footprints of a multi-level airport collected from available sources and displayed on user receivers for orientation [15]. The simulated scenario includes two terminal intersections with four-way arms and moving lanes, along with sidewalks and areas for shopping, dining, or resting. Traffic management involves directing carriers along cardinal points using road request and response segments, exclusive passenger lanes, waiting areas, and crosswalks. Central traffic light systems controlled by a Central Manager regulate carrier flow and prevent collisions. Pedestrians on sidewalks have the freedom to move in both directions. It's a prerequisite that destinations can be targeted by user requests to the CM within a specific request distance (D/P2I) and any floor changes notified if applicable. The indoor route throughout the airport is communicated to the user via a responding message (message distance range; I2D/P) transmitted by the traffic signals, which also function as routers or mesh/cellular nodes (refer to Figure 2).

This request/response framework provides landmark-based instructions to help carriers identify decision points where a change of direction is necessary (action). Furthermore, it offers information to users to confirm that they are on the correct path. The Simulated scenario and environment with the optical infrastructure (X_{ij}), the generated footprints (1-9) and the connected luggage and pedestrians' flow are displayed in Figure 3a. In Figure 3b the schematic diagram of Terminal 2 with coded lanes (L/0-7) and traffic lights (TL/0-15) is draft.

Pedestrians on sidewalks have the freedom to move in both directions. It's a prerequisite that destinations can be targeted by user requests to the CM within a specific request distance (D/P2I) and any floor changes notified if applicable. The indoor route throughout the airport is communicated to the user via a responding message (message distance range; I2D/P) transmitted by the traffic signals, which also function as routers or mesh/cellular nodes (refer to Figure 2).

This request/response framework provides landmark-based instructions to help carriers identify decision points where a change of direction is necessary (action). Furthermore, it offers information to users to confirm that they are on the correct path.

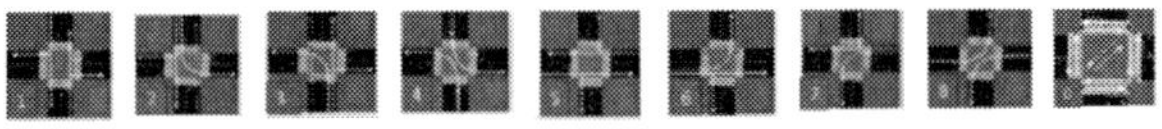

Figure 4. Schematic of a one cycle phase diagram with eight moving walkway phases and an exclusive pedestrian phase.

Figure 4 visually outlines intersection phase progressions (actions) within a structured cycle length, comprising eight AGV carrier phases in the lanes and an exclusive pedestrian phase for the walking passengers. Each phase is subdivided into discrete time sequences, providing a comprehensive temporal framework.

IV. Results

In this section, the algorithms developed for guiding users through indoor spaces are described. Explanation of turn-by-turn directions, landmark highlighting, alerts, and alternate route suggestions are given. Figure 5a displays the decoded optical signals (at the top of the figures) and the signals received (MUX) by the receivers in a D2D (COM 2) and D2I (COM 3) communication scenario involving a leader device in the moving walkway at position ($R_{3,10}$, $G_{3,11}$, $B_{4,10}$). This device is communicating with the CM at the second terminal (T2) on lane L0 (direction E) at 10:25:46 and is followed by three other devices (nr) D_1, D_2, and D_3 with the same direction, located at positions (IDx,y) $R_{3,8}$, $G_{3,6}$ and $R_{3,4}$, respectively.

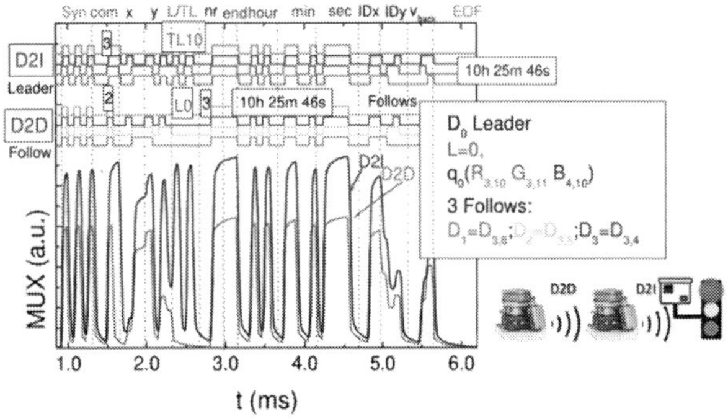

a)

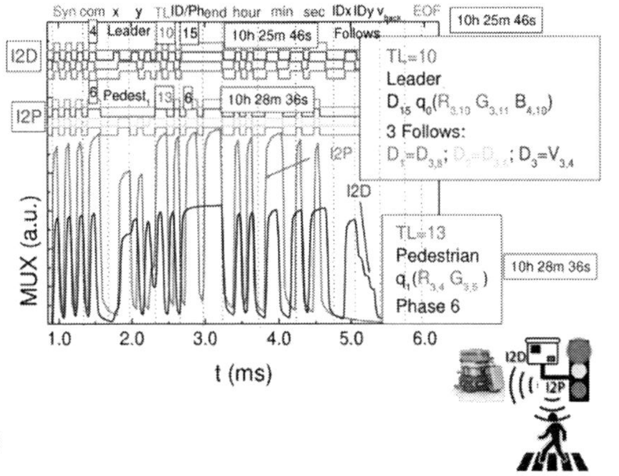

b)

Figure 5. MUX signal request (a) and responses (b) assigned to different types of V-VLC communication. On the top the decoded messages are displayed.

In Figure 5b, the responses (I2D and I2P) from two traffic lights (TL10 and TL13) to the crossing request from the preceding carrier d_o ($R_{3,10}$, $G_{3,11}$, $B_{4,10}$) and a pedestrian q_1 located in the "waiting corner" of the first terminal ($R_{3,4}$, $G_{3,5}$) are exemplified. The timestamps "10:25:46" and "10:28:36" represent the times at which the two responses were sent respectively for the pedestrian (COM 6) and for the Passenger/luggage carrier (COM 4) and provide a reference point for when each response was generated.

Assessing the effectiveness of the proposed V-VLC system in multi-terminal airports utilizes the Simulation of Urban MObility (SUMO), employing agent-based simulations. SUMO serves as a powerful tool for optimizing traffic operations within airports, enhancing efficiency, safety, and passenger experience.

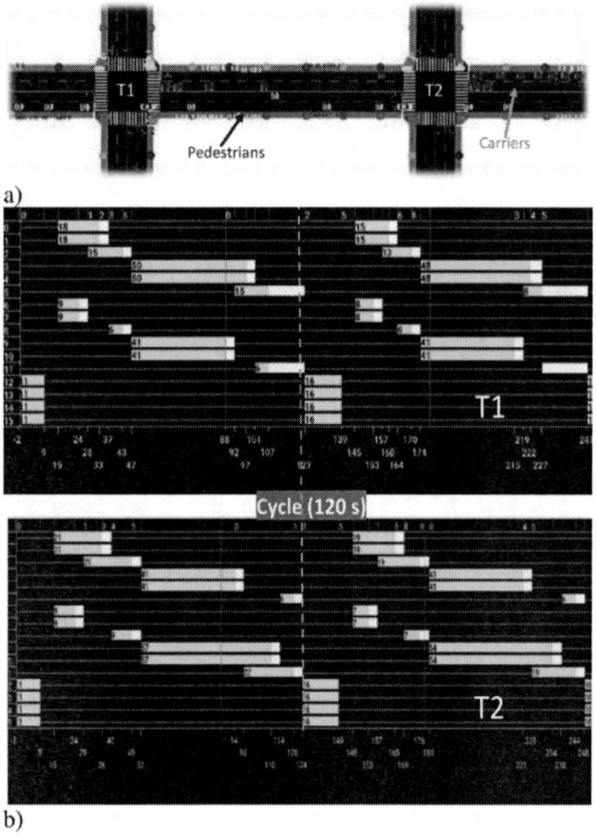

Figure 6. a) SUMO environment. b) State phasing diagram.

SUMO simulates vehicles, pedestrians, and entities in the airport environment, adjusting parameters like traffic density and road layouts. It tests traffic control algorithms, manages intersections, and oversees pedestrian crossings, mirroring real-world airport conditions.

Moreover, SUMO's API supports interaction with external programs, enabling the extraction of diverse traffic flow statistics. State and phase diagrams within SUMO offer insights into traffic signal dynamics and movements within the terminals. The simulation operates on an agent-based system, where agents accumulate experience to navigate traffic situations effectively. They control Traffic Lights (TL) based on decisions aimed at optimizing traffic flow, whether in walkway lanes or sidewalks [16][17].

For data analysis, SUMO collects and analyzes simulation data, including vehicle trajectories, travel times, congestion levels, and pedestrian movements. Visualization capabilities aid in analysis and decision-making, while SUMO's API supports interaction with external programs for diverse traffic flow statistics. Gate assignment approaches for aircraft movement are outlined, aiming to minimize pedestrian walking distances or maximize passenger throughput. Traffic scenarios with varying cycle durations and carrier flows were considered, integrating pedestrian flows to reflect realistic scenarios.

Two potential approaches to gate assignment for aircraft movement, including landings and takeoffs, are outlined: The first approach involves a low carrier flow, accommodating 1800 carriers per hour. Assumptions include a carrier velocity of 9 km/h, primarily moving from east and west directions. The primary objective is to minimize the total pedestrian walking distance inside the terminal. The second approach adopts a high carrier flow, accommodating 2300 carriers per hour at the same velocity. Here, the aim is to maximize the number of passengers served by gates. Both scenarios maintain a consistent pedestrian flow of 11200 per hour. Within these flows, it is expected that 20% of passengers/luggage carriers will turn (remain in the same terminal), while 75% will continue straight (change terminal).

In the airport context, two traffic scenarios were evaluated. The first scenario, termed the High traffic scenario, has cycle duration of 120 seconds and is capable of dispatching 2300 carriers per hour. The second scenario, with a cycle duration of 88 seconds, dispatches 1800 carriers per hour. In Figure 6 the high traffic scenario State phasing diagram. illustrated.

For each terminal, pedestrian flows were simulated with 7200 pedestrians at Terminal T1 and 4000 pedestrians at Terminal T2. Pedestrians were introduced exclusively on the N and S roads in both directions, starting at various distances from the intersection. This setup aims to replicate a more realistic scenario where pedestrians originate from different points, reflecting varied starting positions and paths within the airport environment.

These diagrams offer insights into the dynamic behavior of traffic light signals and carrier/pedestrian movements within the simulated terminals. As can be observed in the diagrams, it is possible to distinguish the different cycles that occur during the simulation. It always begins with a pedestrian phase (Phase 0), during which some individuals can cross the crosswalk, turning red for pedestrians starting from 11 seconds. Then, phases dedicated to carriers (Phases 1-8) take place until it concludes at 123 seconds. At this moment, the second cycle begins, with the pedestrian phase becoming active again. The same process repeats until 247 seconds, marking the end of this second cycle and the initiation of a third cycle. These diagrams align with the analysis conducted for pedestrians.

V. CONCLUSIONS AND FUTURE WORK

Utilizing VLC signals offers a promising solution for enhancing indoor navigation in multi-terminal airports. Integrating VLC with existing lighting infrastructure and traffic control algorithms significantly improves pedestrian and carrier traffic management. By optimizing traffic flow, minimizing pedestrian walking distances, and providing real-time guidance, VLC-based systems enhance accessibility and efficiency in airport environments.

This study developed a two-terminal airport model based on Edge/Fog architecture, established communication protocols, and tested VLC algorithms. These algorithms effectively transmit encoded messages, enabling accurate localization and positioning, and reliable communication between traffic signals and user devices. Real-time guidance provides turn-by-turn directions, highlights landmarks, and suggests alternate routes, thus improving traffic flow management and operational efficiency.

SUMO simulations offer valuable insights into pedestrian behavior and traffic dynamics, revealing the impact of traffic flow, road length, and cycle durations on pedestrian movement. This comprehensive analysis underscores the potential of VLC-based systems in optimizing airport navigation and enhancing overall user experience.

While this study has demonstrated the potential of VLC-based systems for improving indoor navigation and traffic management in multi-terminal airports, several areas warrant further investigation and development:

- Future research should focus on scaling the VLC system to accommodate larger and more complex airport environments. This includes adapting the system to varying architectural designs and passenger volumes to ensure consistent performance.
- Investigating the integration of VLC with other emerging technologies such as 5G, IoT devices, and advanced AI algorithms could further enhance the system's capabilities. Combining these technologies could improve data processing speeds, accuracy, and overall system intelligence.

By addressing these areas, future work can build on the current findings to develop more robust, efficient, and user-friendly VLC-based navigation and traffic management systems for airports.

ACKNOWLEDGEMENTS

This work was sponsored by FCT – Fundação para a Ciência e a Tecnologia, within the Research Unit CTS – Center of Technology and Systems, reference UIDB/00066/2020 and by IPL project reference IPL/IDI&CA2024/NUTRAMISEL.

REFERENCES

[1] E. Ozgur, E. Dinc, and O. B. Akan, "Communicate to illuminate: State-of-the-art and research challenges for visible light communications," Physical Communication 17 pp. 72–85, 2015.

[2] K. Panta and J. Armstrong, "Indoor localisation using white LEDs," Electron. Lett. 48(4), pp. 228–230, 2012.

[3] T. Komiyama, K. Kobayashi, K. Watanabe, T. Ohkubo, and Y. Kurihara, "Study of visible light communication system using RGB LED lights," in Proceedings of SICE Annual Conference, IEEE, pp. 1926–1928, 2011.

[4] Y. Wang, N. Chi, J. Yu, and H. Shang, "Demonstration of 575-Mb/s downlink and 225-Mb/s uplink bi-directional SCM-WDM visible light communication using RGB LED and phosphor-based LED," Opt. Express 21(1), pp.1203–1208, 2013.

[5] D. Tsonev et al., "A 3-Gb/s single-LED OFDM-based wireless VLC link using a Gallium Nitride μLED," IEEE Photon. Technol. Lett. 26(7), pp. 637–640. 2014.

[6] D. O'Brien et al., "Indoor visible light communications: challenges and prospects," Proc. SPIE 7091, 709106, 2008.

[7] E. Monteiro and S. Hranilovic, "Constellation design for color-shift keying using interior point methods," in Proc. IEEE Globecom Workshops, Dec., pp.1224–1228, 2012.

[8] M. Vieira et al., "Three Transducers Embedded into One Single SiC Photodetector: LSP Direct Image Sensor, Optical Amplifier and Demux Device" Advances in Photodiodes in Tech, Chap.19, pp. 403-425, 2011.

[9] M. A. Vieira, P. Louro, M. Vieira, A. Fantoni, and A. Steiger-Garção,"Light-activated amplification in Si-C tandem devices: A capacitive active filter model" IEEE sensor journal, 12, no. 6, pp. 1755-1762, 2012.

[10] A. Jovicic, J. Li, and T. Richardson, "Visible light communication: opportunities, challenges and the path to market," Communications Magazine, IEEE, vol. 51, no. 12, pp. 26–32, 2013.

[11] S T. Komine and M. Nakagawa, "Fundamental analysis for visible-light communication system using led lights," Consumer Electronics, IEEE Transactions on, vol. 50, no. 1, pp. 100–107, 2004.

[12] M. Vieira, M. A. Vieira, P. Louro, P. Vieira, and A. Fantoni, "Light-emitting diodes aided indoor localization using visible light communication technology," Opt. Eng. 57(8), 087105, 2018.

[13] M. A. Vieira, G. Galvão, M. Vieira, P. Louro, M. Vestias, P. Vieira, "Enhancing Urban Intersection Efficiency: Visible Light Communication and Learning-Based Control for Traffic Signal Optimization and Vehicle Management." Symmetry 2024, 16, 240. https://doi.org/10.3390/ sym16020240.

[14] M. Vieira, M. A. Vieira, P. Louro, A. Fantoni, P. Vieira, "Dynamic VLC navigation system in Crowded Buildings", International Journal on Advances in Software, vol. 14 no. 3&4, pp. pp. 141-150, 2021.

[15] M. Vieira, M. A. Vieira, P. Vieira, and P. Louro "Enhancing Building Guidance: A Visible Light Communication-based Identifier (ID) System," Sensors & Transducers Journal, vol. 263, issue 4, pp. 74-81, December 2023.

[16] M. Vieira, M. A. Vieira, P. Louro, A. Fantoni, and P. Vieira, "A System for Indoor Guidance Using Visible Light Communication" International Journal on Advances in Networks and Services, vol. 15 no. 3 & 4, year 2022, ISSN: 1942-2644, pp.35-45, December 31, 2022.

[17] M. Vieira, M. A. Vieira, G. Galvão, P. Louro, P. Vieira, and A. Fantoni, "Enhancing Indoor Navigation in Multi-Terminal Airports through Visible Light Communication Signals," Proc. SPIE 12999, Optical Sensing and Detection VIII, 129991N, June 2024.

Mobility of Autonomous Guided Vehicles Supported by Visible Light Communication

Paula Louro, Gonçalo Galvão, Manuela Vieira, Manuel Augusto Vieira
DEETC/ISEL/IPL, R. Conselheiro Emídio Navarro, 1959-007
Lisboa, Portugal

CTS-UNINOVA-LASI
Quinta da Torre, Monte da Caparica, 2829-516,
Caparica, Portugal

e-mail: paula.louro@isel.pt, a45903@alunos.isel.pt, mv@isel.pt, mvieira@deetc.isel.pt

Abstract— **This paper explores Autonomous Guided Vehicles (AGV) mobility in dense industrial environments, utilizing Visible Light Communication (VLC) technology for data transmission between infrastructures and vehicles, establishing X2X links. Tetrachromatic white Light Emitting Diodes (LEDs) and dedicated pinpin photodiodes facilitate simultaneous lighting and data transmission, while VLC-based indoor positioning enables guidance services with tailored coding schemes for each link. By analyzing AGV flow regulation within warehouse lanes similar to urban traffic flow, an urban mobility simulator generates movement data. A dynamic model integrating VLC queuing/request/response behaviors, efficiently schedules routes, ensuring optimal travel and avoiding congestion. The proof-of-concept is demonstrated through evaluations of travel time and traffic flows.**

Keywords- Visible Light Communication; positioning; guidance system; mobility; autonomous guided vehicle.

I. Introduction

Autonomous Guided Vehicles (AGVs) are driverless carts widely utilized in industrial and distribution settings for material movement [1]. AGVs streamline operations across various industries, enhancing inventory management, production flexibility, and staff efficiency. They facilitate data-driven analytics, predictive maintenance, and reliability improvement. Originally used in manufacturing, AGVs now serve diverse industrial applications including warehouse logistics and container terminal operations [2]. Some AGVs feature robotic arms or serve as collaborative robots (cobots), extending their functionality to tasks like picking and assembly AGVs are prominent in automotive, logistics, e-commerce, food, pharmaceuticals, and more [3].

The rapid adoption of Autonomous Guided Vehicles (AGVs) in industrial environments has increased the need for efficient and reliable communication systems. While traditional wireless technologies such as Wi-Fi and Radio Frequency (RF) are widely used, they face challenges in dense industrial settings due to signal interference, limited bandwidth, and security vulnerabilities. Visible Light Communication (VLC) presents a promising alternative, offering high-speed data transmission with minimal interference and enhanced security [4]. However, there is limited research on integrating VLC into AGV systems, particularly in highly congested environments where signal reliability and uninterrupted communication are crucial for operational efficiency. This research aims to address this gap by exploring the potential of VLC to optimize AGV mobility and coordination in dense industrial environments, providing a novel approach to improving communication reliability and overall system performance [5].

VLC technology [6] enhances AGV collaboration in dense industrial environments by providing accurate indoor positioning and mapping. LED light sources are modulated to encode data, offering advantages like high-speed transmission, immunity to electromagnetic interference, and enhanced security. The dense deployment of VLC transmitters makes it ideal for indoor localization and navigation [6][7].

This paper discusses the integrated movement of AGVs performing tasks in indoor environments. AGV fleet management treats their movements similar to vehicular traffic, controlled by intelligent agents based on congestion conditions [8][9]. Vehicular communication relies on visible links, facilitating Lamp-to-Vehicle (L2V), Vehicle-to-Vehicle (V2V), Vehicle-to-Infrastructure (V2I), and Infrastructure-to-Vehicle (I2V) channels [10].

In this work, VLC technology is employed to create an indoor positioning system with additional communication capabilities. The system includes a pinpin heterostructure a:SiC:H device for photodetection of optical signals emitted by white trichromatic RGB LEDs. The photodetector [11][12], which is based on a-SiC:H/a-Si:H heterostructures, operates in the visible spectrum. It features active filtering and amplification properties, as well as selective sensitivity, designed to be wavelength-sensitive [14][15]. When different visible signals are encoded along the same optical transmission path, the device multiplexes these optical channels, performs various filtering processes (such as amplification, switching, and wavelength conversion), and outputs a multiplexed signal. Decoding this signal allows for the recovery of the modulated signal transmitted by each emitter [13].

The proposed system is modelled using the Simulation of Urban Mobility (SUMO) [14], with a dynamic algorithm effectively scheduling AGV routes [15][16]. Simulation experiments validate the method's efficiency in travel and congestion avoidance, as demonstrated in [15], that uses a similar methodology to optimize urban intersections by integrating VLC localization services with learning-based traffic signal control.

The indoor localization system combines optical wireless communication, computer algorithms, smart sensors, and an optical sources network, constituting a collaborative cyber-physical system approach.

The paper is organized as follows. Section I includes the paper introduction with related work. Section II outlines the VLC system specifications, including details on the transmitter and receiver, indoor positioning and guidance-based services and VLC protocols. In Section III, the experimental scenarios are described, along with a presentation and discussion of the obtained results. Finally, Section IV concludes the paper and offers guidelines for future work.

II. ARCHITECTURE OF THE VLC SYSTEM

The communication network uses four different VLC Channels ensuring communication Lamp-to-Vehicle (L2V), Vehicle-to-Vehicle (V2V), Vehicle-to-Infrastructure (V2I) and Infrastructure-to-Vehicle (I2V), as illustrated in Figure 1.

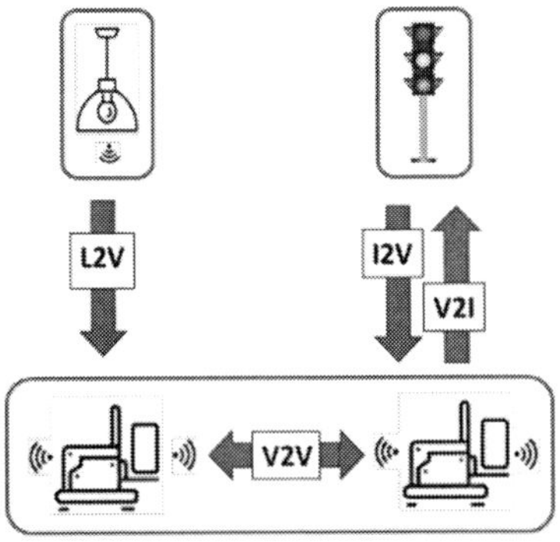

Figure 1. Communication channels established using visible signals.

A. VLC Transmitter and Receiver

The VLC system utilizes tetra-chromatic white LEDs, with each LED containing independently controllable red, green, and blue emitters. This configuration enables the creation of distinct data transmission channels by controlling each emitter separately. A single L2V transmitter comprises four LEDs arranged in a square formation, with only one emitter from each LED utilized for transmission. In V2V and V2I communication, only a single LED emitter is used. These tetra-chromatic LEDs emit distinct wavelengths in the red (620 nm), green (530 nm), blue (470 nm), and violet (405 nm) bands. These LEDs meet illumination standards, making them suitable for lighting and communication. Their effective channel separation and wide coverage area make them ideal for communication applications.

The VLC receiver features pinpin photodiodes with a-SiC:H/a-Si:H heterostructures, optimized for modulated wavelengths from RGB LEDs in the visible range. Its sensitivity is influenced by external optical bias, favoring short wavelengths under back violet background illumination and longer wavelengths under front illumination. The device acts as both a short-pass filter for back illumination and a long-pass filter for front illumination, with tuning options for short, medium, and long spectral regions. Front illumination enhances the red spectrum, while back illumination boosts the blue signal.

B. Indoor positioning and guidance based services

Indoor positioning with VLC uses L2V communication, where LEDs in ceiling lamps are arranged in a square configuration, defining unit navigation cells. Each cell is divided into footprints, assigned to different optical excitations. Figure 2 depicts the L2V transmitter configuration, unit navigation cell, and corresponding footprints. Footprint regions (#1, #2, ..., #9) correspond to optical excitations shown in Figure 2. Matrix notation identifies each emitter in the VLC transmitter network, transmitting data to determine navigation cell positions.

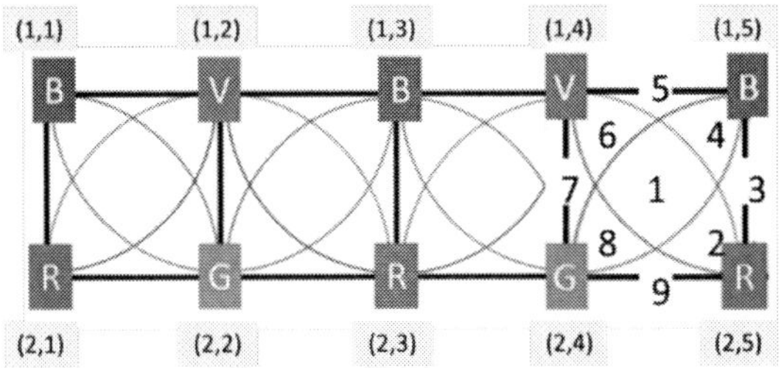

Figure 2. Square configuration of VLC transmitters of the L2V link showing the unit navigation cell and footprints inside the unit navigation cell.

Each L2V VLC transmitter uniquely identifies its position within the indoor space, defining navigation cells. Within each cell, resolution is enhanced by measuring optical patterns, resulting in 9 distinct regions. Vehicle guidance along lanes and directional changes are facilitated by transmitting respective directions via the I2V link.

C. VLC Protocols

Data transmission requires a specific modulation scheme. We use On-Off Keying (OOK), valued for its simplicity in VLC systems. In OOK modulation, the presence of a signal is represented by one level (usually the "on" state), while the absence of a signal is represented by another level (usually the "off" state). In other words, the carrier signal is switched on and off to represent digital data.

The communication protocol, outlined in Table I, controls information exchange, including synchronization, identification, and payload sections within each transmitted frame. The frame structure is systematic and standardized, with variations based on the type of communication (1-4: 1-L2V, 2-V2V, 3-V2I, 4-I2V). Each frame is 64 bits long, featuring specific blocks at the beginning and end to support synchronization of successive data frames.

TABLE I - CODIFICATION PROTOCOLS.

L2V	SYNC	1	x	y	END	h	m	s	Payload							EOF
V2V	SYNC	2	x	y	Lane (0-7)	#AVG	END	h	m	s	x'	y'	#N	Payload		EOF
V2I	SYNC	3	x	y	TL (0-15)	#AVG	END	h	m	s	x'	y'	#N	Payload		EOF
I2V	SYNC	4	x	y	TL (0-15)	ID-AVG	END	h	m	s	x'	y'	#N	phase	Payload	EOF

The data frame consists of modular blocks, each comprising 4 bits, except for SYNC and timeline-related blocks (h-hour, m-minute, s-second), which use 5 bits each. Each VLC link's coding begins and ends with SoH and EOF blocks ([10101] and [0000], respectively), ensuring synchronization. The transmitter's position is coded as x and y in matrixial notation, while timeline details are coded as {END, h, m, s} ([111] for END). Other codes include Lane, TL, #AGV, x' and y', ID-AVG, and #N, facilitating effective encoding and decoding of AGV movement information. This protocol guarantees synchronization and data integrity in VLC communication.

At the receiver, the photodetector generates a multiplexed signal based on input optical signals. With the VLC transmitter's 4 independent emitters, the output signals can combine one to four optical excitations, yielding 16 photocurrent levels. Bit decoding corresponds to assigning each photocurrent level to the respective optical excitation, achieved through previous system calibration to adjust photocurrent levels.

III. RESULTS AND DISCUSSION

A. AGV Traffic Scenario

Inside the warehouse, AGVs navigate corridors to pick up goods from predefined aisles. AGV flow is determined by assigned routes and stop times for aisle operations. AGVs adhere to right-hand traffic rules, using right lanes for forward and right turns, and left lanes exclusively for left turns. Tasks begin at the charging station, with AGVs following their routes until reaching the packaging station. AGVs can start operations from the packaging station while charging, upon receiving new collection instructions. The simulated scenario, depicted in Figure 3, comprises multi-intersections with two 4-way intersections having 2 lanes per arm.

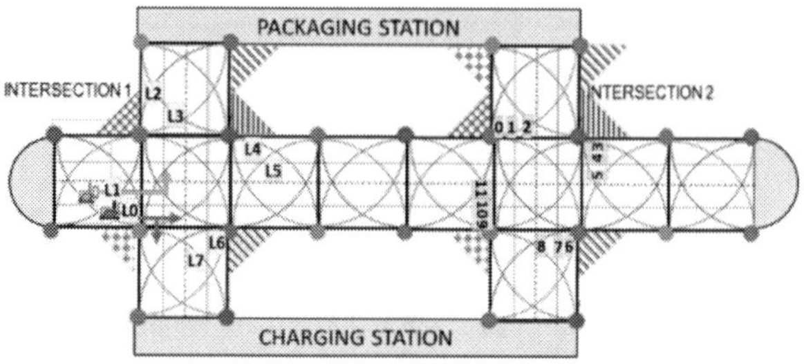

Figure 3. Lanes and aisles inside the warehouse.

Central traffic light systems, managed by Central Managers (CMs), control traffic flow. Four traffic flows along cardinal points are considered, with binary choices (turn left/straight or turn right) in road request and response segments. In intersection 1, even lanes (L0, L2, L4, L6) enable right turns or forward movements, while odd lanes allow left turns. Unit navigation cells defined by optical transmitters in the L2V channel are depicted along corridors, along with respective footprints. Each intersection has three traffic lights for possible movements (forward, turn left/right) in the convergent lane, totalling 12 traffic lights per intersection (TL0, TL1, ..., TL11). Intersection 2 displays corresponding traffic lights, regulating flows from north to south (TL0, TL1, TL2), east to west (TL3, TL4, TL5), south to north (TL6, TL7, TL8), and west to east (TL9, TL10, TL11). Traffic lights are ordered by turns, with lower orders for right turns (TL0, TL3, TL6, TL9), higher for left turns (TL2, TL5, TL8, TL11), and intermediate for forward movements (TL1, TL4, TL7, TL10).

B. VLC signals

Using the described spatial layout, optical communication was simulated with multiple AGVs moving eastward along lane L0, as depicted in Figure 4. The foremost AGV in the lane, located at position $R_{3,10}$ (x and y in matrix notation), communicates with the intersection agent via V2I communication. It transmits a request for forward movement at the intersection and communicates the number and positions of trailing AGVs (AVG1, AVG2, and AVG3), occupying positions $R_{3,8}$, $R_{3,6}$, and $R_{3,4}$ simultaneously.

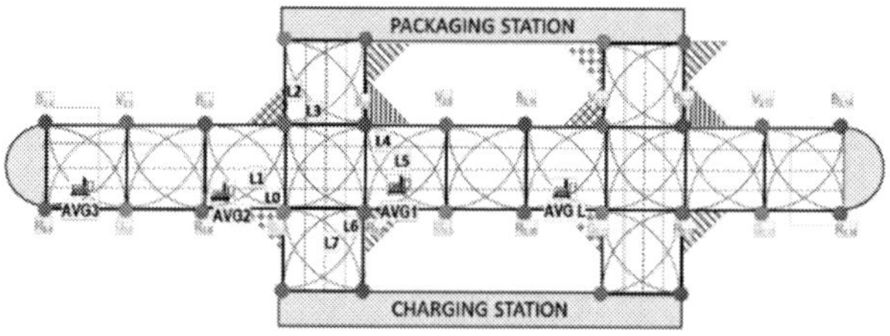

Figure 4. Simulation scenario.

Using the communication protocol defined in Table I, the VLC system was configured to establish data transmission from each link. The optical signals measured at the receivers of links V2I and V2V are displayed in Figure 5. The transmitted optical signals from each transmitter are represented on the top of the figure.

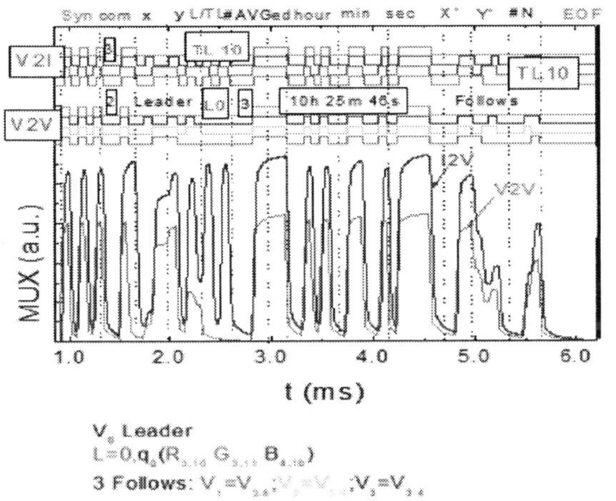

Figure 5. Experimental data acquired by the receiver of the V2V and V2I VLC links.

In the I2V link, the leading AGV transmits a bit sequence following the protocol in Table I. The receiver detects different signal levels, each corresponding to a specific input combination. Decoding these levels using appropriate calibration signals allows recovery of the input optical signals. The frame begins with synchronization bits, followed by communication type (3 for V2I), position ($R_{3,10}$, $G_{3,11}$,$B_{4,10}$), intersection movement request (TL = 10 for forward movement), communication time (10:25:46), number of AGVs behind in the lane (3), and their coordinates: (3,8) for AVG1, (3,6) for AVG2, and (3,4) for AVG3, transmitted by red, green, and blue transmitters. In the V2V link, the leading AGV transmits synchronization bits, communication type (2 for V2V), position ($R_{3,10}$, $G_{3,11}$,$B_{4,10}$),movement lane (L = 0 for forward or right turn), communication time (10:25:46), number of AGVs behind in the same lane (3), and their coordinates: (3,8) for AVG1, (3,6) for AVG2, and (3,4) for AVG3.

Figure 6 displays the optical signals acquired by the receiver of the I2V VLC link at the second intersection. The transmitted optical signals from each transmitter are represented on the top of the figure.

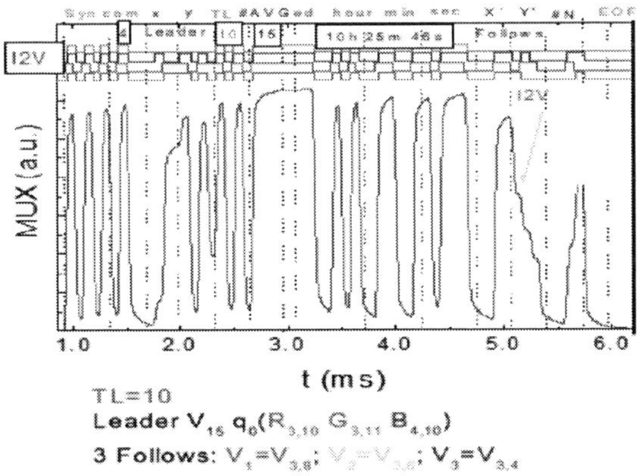

Figure 6. Experimental data acquired by the receiver of the I2V VLC link located at intersection #2.

In this communication, the block after the synchronization bits, define an I2V communication (ID=4), followed by the identification of the corresponding traffic light (TL=10), the identification of the leading AGV (15 in this case), the communication time and the number of leading AGV's followers (3), and respective coordinates: (3,8), (3,6) and (3,4). This is in accordance with the information transmitted by the AVG L.

C. Dynamic Traffic Model

AGV flow dynamics were assessed using SUMO, an open-source traffic simulation package for large networks. The simulation configured the scenario previously described and evaluated average speed and halting over a fixed period (one hour). Figure 7 and Figure 8 compare the average speeds and halting trends over time for low and high traffic AGV scenarios, assuming flows of 1800 and 2300 AGVs per hour, respectively.

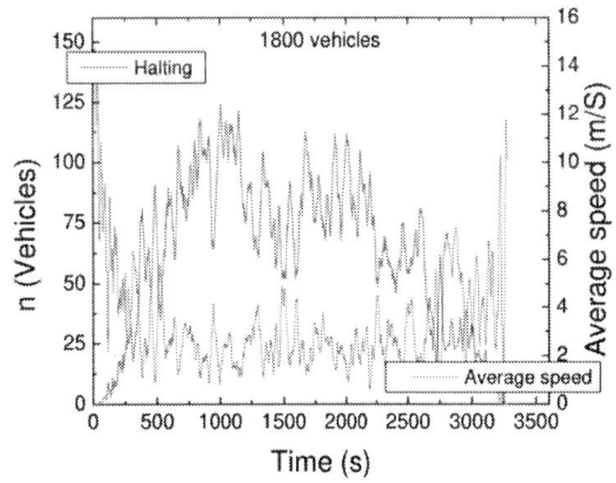

Figure 7. Average speed and halting in low traffic AGV scenario, 1800 AGV/hour.

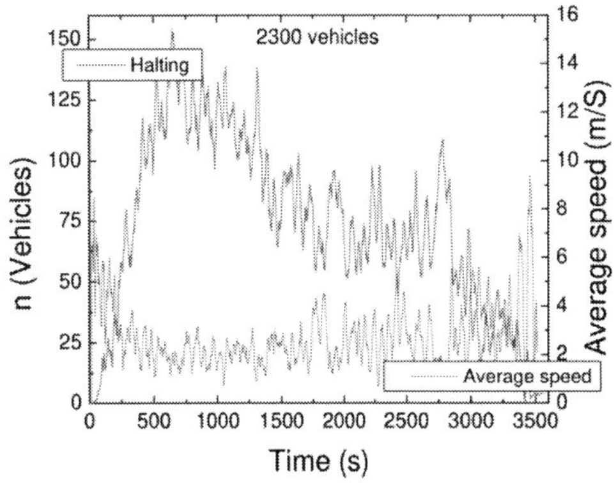

Figure 8. Average speed and halting in high traffic AGV scenario, 2300 AGV/hour.

Data from Figure 7 and Figure 8 show an initial spike in speed at the start of halting simulations, gradually decreasing as the simulation progresses. This acceleration is due to fewer AGVs at intersections, allowing faster movement. However, as more AGVs enter the system, average speed notably drops until the end of the simulation. As AGVs empty out, remaining ones have more space, leading to increased speed due to reduced congestion. Higher waiting AGV volumes correspond to decreased speed, while lower volumes result in increased speed, aligning with traffic dynamics expectations. The proof-of-concept evaluations demonstrated the feasibility of the approach using key metrics like travel time and traffic flow. However, these preliminary results were not tested for statistical significance. Future work will include larger-scale experiments to ensure statistical validation.

IV. CONCLUSIONS

The proposed application monitors and manages AGV movement in an optimized warehouse for material collection and transport. VLC links facilitate AGV flow, reducing congestion and waiting times. Various coding protocols were defined for VLC links, with experimental data obtained for V2V, V2I, and I2V links. Using the SUMO simulator, the same scenario was analyzed as urban traffic flow, considering low and high flows to simulate average speed and halting trends over a period. Results can predict traffic actions, prevent congestion, and reduce travel time, enhancing collection and transportation efficiency.

The paper presents a proof-of-concept of the use of Visible Light Communication (VLC) in combination with AGV (Automated Guided Vehicle) mobility The practical implementation of such a system in a real industrial environment might pose significant challenges, which must be addressed in future work, namely, scalability, cost, and potential obstacles to real-world deployment.

ACKNOWLEDGMENT

This work was sponsored by FCT – Fundação para a Ciência e a Tecnologia, within the Research Unit CTS – Center of Technology and systems, reference UIDB/00066/2020 and IPL/2024/INUTRAM_ISEL.

REFERENCES

[1] F. Gul, S. Sahal Nazli Alhady, and W. Rahiman, "A review of controller approach for autonomous guided vehicle system", Indonesian Journal of Electrical Engineering and Computer Science, vol. 20, no.1, pp. 552-562, 2020. DOI: 10.11591/ijeecs.v20.i1.pp552-562.

[2] K. J. Roodbergen, and I. F. Vis, "A survey of literature on automated storage and retrieval systems," European Journal of Operational Research, vol. 194, no. 2, pp. 343-362, 2009.

[3] P. C. Hsiao, and S. L. Chang, "The application of Automated Guided Vehicles (AGVs) in different manufacturing systems: A literature review." Procedia CIRP, vol. 81, pp. 570-575, 2019.

[4] P. Louro, M. Vieira, and M. A. Vieira, "Geolocalization and navigation by visible light communication to address automated logistics control," Opt. Eng. vol. 6, no. 1, 016104, 2022. DOI:10.1117/1.OE.61.1.016104.

[5] A. M. Căilean and M. Dimian, "Current Challenges for Visible Light Communications Usage in Vehicle Applications: A Survey". IEEE Communications Surveys & Tutorials, vol. 19, no. 4, pp. 2681-2703, 2017. doi: 10.1109/COMST.2017.2706940 364.

[6] M.. F. Keskin, A.D. Sezer, and S. Gezici, "Localization via Visible Light Systems", Proceedings of the IEEE, vol. 1006, no. 6, pp. 1063–1088, 2018. DOI:10.1109/JPROC.2018.2823500

[7] Y. Zhuang et al., "A Survey of Positioning Systems Using Visible LED Lights". IEEE Communications Surveys Tutorials, vol. 20, pp. 1963–1988, 2018.

[8] S. Caputo et al., ''Measurement-based VLC channel characterization for I2V communications in a real urban scenario,'' Vehicular Communications, vol. 28, pp. 100305, 2021. DOI:10.1016/j.vehcom.2020.100305

[9] M. A. Vieira, M. Vieira, P. Vieira, and P. Louro, "Optical signal processing for a smart vehicle lighting system using a-SiCH technology," Proc. SPIE 10231, Optical Sensors 2017, 102311L, 2017.

[10] P. Louro, M. Vieira, and M. A. Vieira, "Bidirectional visible light communication," Opt. Eng. vol. 59, no. 12, 127109, 2020. DOI: 10.1117/1.OE.59.12.127109.

[11] M. A. Vieira, M. Vieira, V. Silva, and P. Louro "Optical signal processing for indoor positioning using a-SiCH technology" Proc. SPIE 9891, Silicon Photonics and Photonic Integrated Circuits V, 98911Z, 2016.

[12] P. Louro et al., "Optical demultiplexer based on an a-SiC:H voltage controlled device", Phys. Status Solidi C vol. 7, no. 3–4, pp. 1188–1191, 2010. DOI: 10.1002/pssc.200982702.

[13] P. Louro, M. Vieira, and M. A. Vieira, "Geolocalization and navigation by visible light communication to address automated logistics control," Opt. Eng. vol. 61, no. 1, 016104, 2022, doi: 10.1117/1.OE.61.1.016104.

[14] M. F. Keskin, A. D. Sezer, and S. Gezici, "Localization via Visible Light Systems". Proceedings of the IEEE 2018, 597 106, pp. 1063–1088. doi:10.1109/JPROC.2018.2823500

[15] M.A Vieira, G. Galvão, M. Vieira, P. Louro, M. Vestias, and P.Vieira, "Enhancing Urban Intersection Efficiency: Visible Light Communication and Learning-Based Control for Traffic Signal Optimization and Vehicle Management". Symmetry, vol. 16, no. 2, pp. 240, 2024. DOI:10.3390/sym16020240.

Research on Structural Health Monitoring of Steel Tower Structure Using Long-term Vibration Sensing

Narito Kurata
Faculty of Industrial Technology
Tsukuba University of Technology
Tsukuba City, Ibaraki, Japan
e-mail: kurata@home.email.ne.jp

Abstract - **Many steel tower structures built in Japan are aging and are increasingly at risk of collapse in the event of typhoons or major earthquakes. At the same time, it is difficult to proceed with rebuilding such aging structures with limited budgets and manpower, thus there is a need to monitor the health of the structures, and to equalize and facilitate the rebuilding work. For this purpose, it is necessary to make full use of sensing technology to diagnose deterioration in order to accurately assess the condition of steel tower structures. In this study, sensors were installed at multiple locations on an actual steel tower structure, and measurements were taken over a period of nine months. Data was measured and saved for five minutes, centered on the time when the maximum Root Mean Square (RMS) value of acceleration occurred each day. There have been no other studies in which measurements were taken and analyzed at the time when the maximum vibration occurred each day, with almost no missing data, over several months of constant measurement. This study aims to obtain knowledge that will be useful for monitoring the health of structures and for leveling and smoothing out reconstruction work in order to prevent loss of life due to the collapse of steel tower structures that have not yet been made apparent.**

Keywords-Vibration Sensing; Steel Tower Structure; Structural Health Monitoring; Micro Electro Mechanical Systems; Frequency Analysis.

I. INTRODUCTION

In Japan, the civil infrastructure is aging, with approximately 60% of road bridges, river management facilities, such as sluice gates, and port quays, among them, being more than 50 years old after construction by 2033. This situation has been pointed out since the early 2000s, but it came to be highlighted as an important social issue after the 2013 Sasago Tunnel ceiling plate fall accident, in which nine people lost their lives when the vehicles they were traveling in became trapped under the fallen ceiling [1]. In a similar context, the maintenance and reconstruction of steel tower structures, which are ubiquitous throughout Japan for communication and power transmission, is one of the most pressing social issues that has yet to be acknowledged. Steel tower structures consist of a steel framework, and are used for power transmission towers, communication towers for mobile phone base stations, and transmission towers for broadcasting stations, as well as watchtowers for weather observations, lighthouses and firefighting. For power transmission alone, there are currently 240,000 towers supporting the electricity supply [2], and along with communication towers, they form the very infrastructure that underpins our social life. The rush to build transmission towers began in the 1970s, and although the average service life of these towers is estimated to be around 40 years, 120,000, or about half of the total, are overdue for renewal. For example, Typhoon No. 15, which hit the Japanese archipelago in September 2019, caused material damage, including the collapse of a transmission tower in Kimitsu, Chiba Prefecture, which was built in the 1970s, but fortunately no human casualties were reported [3]. For this reason, the importance of this social issue, as regards the maintenance and management of infrastructure as tunnels and bridges, has not yet been recognized. Clearly, many steel towers have reached the point where they need renewal, and the risk of collapse in the event of a typhoon or major earthquake is increasing. It is difficult, however, to renew of all of them at once with limited budgets and manpower, there is an urgent need to monitor their health and extend their service life, as well as to equalize and facilitate reconstruction work. It is therefore essential to accurately assess the condition of steel towers, and to diagnose deterioration using sensing and digital technology.

We have been researching and developing sensing systems that achieve highly accurate autonomous time synchronization for structural health monitoring and earthquake observation. In the light of the current situation, this study collected and analyzed measurement data over several months by installing sensors on a real steel tower in service to obtain knowledge useful for monitoring the health of towers and extending their service life, as well as for equalizing and facilitating reconstruction work, thereby to prevent loss of human life due to unforeseen tower collapse.

Section II describes the state of the art of the research for structural health monitoring and sensor technologies. Section III describes the targeted steel tower structure and the installed sensing system, while Section IV presents the results of an analysis of the measured data. From these results, Section V presents the conclusions of the study and future tasks.

II. STATE OF THE ART

Many studies on the health monitoring of structures have been conducted since the early 2000s, and papers summarizing research trends at that time have been published. Techniques and methodologies for monitoring of structures have been summarized, focusing on the modeling of structural behavior, data analysis methods and sensor technologies [4][5]. Many of the studies focus on social infrastructure structures, such as bridges and highways, where inspections are mandatory, and technologies, such as fiber-optic sensors, wireless sensor networks and image processing have been applied [6][7]. In recent years, machine learning has been utilized in this field, and efforts have been made to apply machine learning algorithms, acquire and process data, and improve prediction capabilities [8]. Moreover, real-time monitoring, data analysis and optimization of maintenance planning have been carried out with regard to structural health monitoring and management systems based on the Internet of Things (IoT) and cloud computing [9]. However, for steel tower structures, inspections are not mandatory and few studies have focused on maintenance management through structural health monitoring. In addition, because transmission towers are owned by electric power companies while communications towers are owned by telecommunications carriers, information on initiatives targeting them is not publicly available. In this study, sensors were installed at multiple locations on an actual steel tower structure, and measurements were taken over a period of nine months. Data was measured and saved for five minutes, centered on the time when the maximum RMS value of acceleration occurred each day. There have been no other studies in which measurements were taken and analyzed at the time when the maximum vibration occurred each day, with almost no missing data, over several months of constant measurement [4][5][6]. This study aims to obtain knowledge that will be useful for monitoring the health of structures and for leveling and smoothing out reconstruction work in order to prevent loss of life due to the collapse of steel tower structures that have not yet been made apparent.

III. STEEL TOWER STRUCTURE AND SENSING SYSTEM

For the many steel towers that require renewal, rather than just focusing on the number of years since construction, it is important to accurately assess their condition in order to monitor the health of individual towers, extend their service life, and equalize and facilitate reconstruction work. To perform such analyses, data must be acquired and collected from actual steel tower structures. Long-term measurements over a period of several months were therefore carried out on a steel tower constructed in Numazu, Shizuoka Prefecture, as shown in Figure 1. Also, it shows the arrangement and types of sensors used. The sensors were placed at the top, center and base of the steel tower in order to obtain data on the overall and local behavior of the tower, which is directly related to any damage it may have sustained.

Table 1 lists the installation location and the measurement data obtained. Accelerometers measure the acceleration at the top, center and base of the tower. Table 2 lists the specifications of the accelerometer. The accelerometer has a 3-axis crystal acceleration sensor with high accuracy and excellent stability, which is micro-fabricated from a highly accurate and stable crystal material.

The sampling frequency was 100 Hz, and data was measured and saved for 5 minutes around the time when the maximum RMS value of acceleration occurred on each day. Each sensor module had a built-in battery and wireless communication function that used the 2.4 GHz frequency band, and transmitted data wirelessly to a data logger for data recording, which was installed at the base shown in Figure 1. The batteries installed in each sensor module can power the system for approximately one year without needing to be replaced. Each sensor module stores data in its memory and transmits the data wirelessly to the logger. The logger was installed in a small temporary structure adjacent to the base of the tower structure and provided with Internet access, allowing data to be collected remotely.

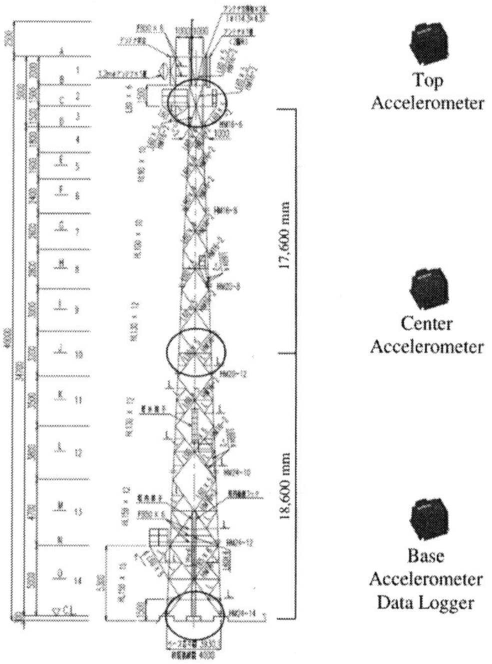

Figure 1. Steel tower structure and sensor location.

TABLE I. INSTALLATION LOCATIONS AND MEASUREMENT DATA OF SENSOR

Sensor	Installation Location	Measurement Data
Accelerometer	Tower top, center, base	Acceleration in two horizontal directions and vertical direction

TABLE II. SPECIFICATIONS OF ACCELEROMETER

Model	EPSON M-A351AS
Direction	3 axes (2 horizontal, 1 vertical)
Range	±5G
Noise Density	0.5 μG/√Hz
Operating Temperature	-20 ℃ to +85 ℃
Power Consumption	20mA
Interface	SPI

IV. DATA ANALYSIS

The accelerometers measured the acceleration at the top, center and base to capture the main vibration modes of the steel tower, and to check for excessive vibration and deformation in each part and between parts. In this study, measurements were taken over a nine-month period from February to October 2023. Data was measured and stored for five minutes, centered on the time when the maximum RMS value of daily acceleration occurred. There have been no other research studies in which measurements were taken almost without missing data at the time when the maximum vibration occurred each day on an actual tower structure, and the results of frequency analysis over several months were presented [4][5][6]. The results below show the long-term changes in the dynamic characteristics of the tower structure.

Figure 2 shows the maximum values measured by accelerometers during the measurement period.

Figure 3 shows the Fourier spectra of the measured data at the top of the tower obtained by an accelerometer during the measurement period. In Figures. 3(a) to (c), the diagrams on the left show the 3D Fourier spectrum with the date and frequency during the nine-month measurement period on the horizontal axis and amplitude plotted on the vertical axis; the diagrams on the right show this spectrum viewed from directly above, with the date and frequency on the axis and the amplitude in color. The white areas in the right diagrams are areas of missing data. The diagrams on the left give an overview of which frequencies were predominant with respect to acceleration at the top of the tower during the nine-month period, and whether these frequencies changed or not. From the diagrams on the right, the predominant frequencies and their changes can be clearly observed. Since this is the acceleration at the top of the tower, the first-order natural frequencies in the horizontal directions of the targeted steel tower can be obtained. From Figure 3(a), in the x-direction, the horizontal natural frequency can be observed at 1.66 Hz, and from (b), in the y-direction, at 1.59 Hz. Also, no change was observed during the nine months when the measurements were conducted. From (c), the natural frequency in the vertical direction (z-direction) can be observed at 42.5 Hz. Natural frequency is the inherent resonant frequency of a structure. It varies depending on the shape, restraint position, and Young's modulus and density of the material. At this frequency, once an external force is applied, the structure resonates and continues to vibrate on its own without the application of an external force. Natural frequency is determined by the mass and stiffness of the structure, so if the structure is damaged, its stiffness decreases and the natural frequency decreases.

Figure 4 shows the Fourier spectra of the measured data obtained at the center of the tower by the accelerometer during the measurement period. Since it is the acceleration at the center, the second-order natural frequencies in the horizontal direction of the targeted steel tower can be obtained. From Figures 4(a) and (b), the dominant frequency is around 6.5 Hz in both the x- and y-directions, but there is no clear peak. It can also be seen that there was no change during the nine months in which the measurements were conducted.

The day when the maximum acceleration occurred is indicated by ▼ in Figure 2. Figure 5 shows the time history waveforms of the data measured at the top of the tower by the accelerometer at this time. From Figure 5, it can be seen that at the top of the tower, accelerations of similar magnitude occur in the x and y-directions, which are horizontal directions, while almost no acceleration occurs in the z-direction, which is the vertical direction. As indicated in (2) above, the natural frequency in the x-direction can be observed at 1.66 Hz, and from (b), the horizontal natural frequency in the y-direction, at 1.59 Hz. In general, there is little structural difference between steel towers in the x- and y-directions, thus the natural frequencies are also close.

Figures 6 and 7 show the time history waveforms and Fourier spectra of the measured data in each direction by the accelerometers on the day when the maximum acceleration of the measurement period occurred. In both the x-direction shown in Figure 6 and the y-direction shown in Figure 7, the base of tower does not vibrate, and the acceleration increases towards the center and the top of the tower, indicating the first-order mode vibrations are dominant, while the higher-order mode vibrations are small. Therefore, the first-order natural frequencies in two horizontal directions are appropriate as a risk indicator for detecting deterioration and damage to steel towers. If there is a change in the risk index, specifically if a trend toward a decrease in the natural frequency is observed, it can be assumed that the stiffness of the structure has decreased, which will lead to an increased priority for detailed inspections and planned reconstruction work.

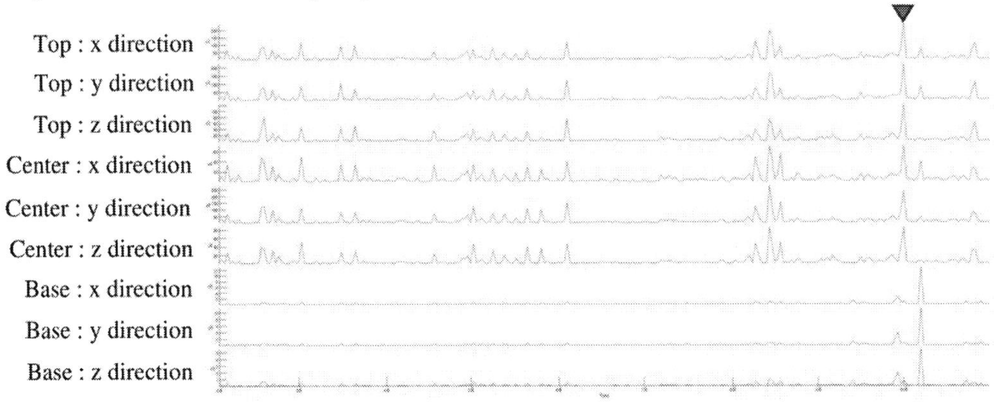

Figure 2. Maximum values measured by accelerometers during the measurement period.

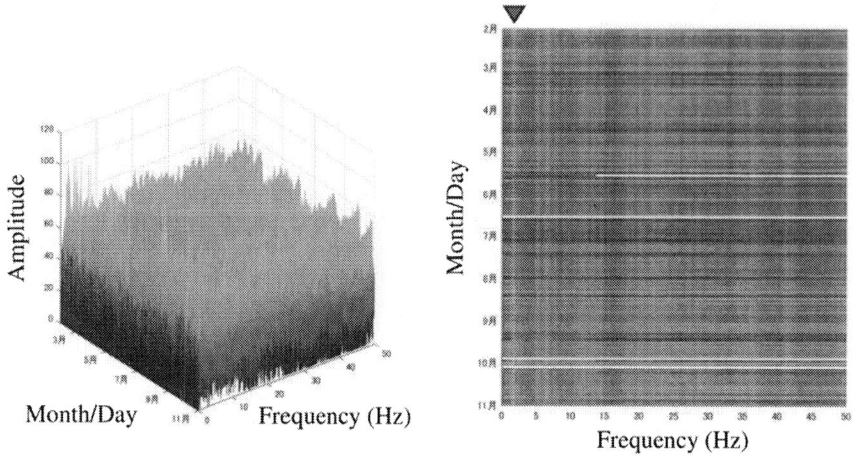

(a) x direction

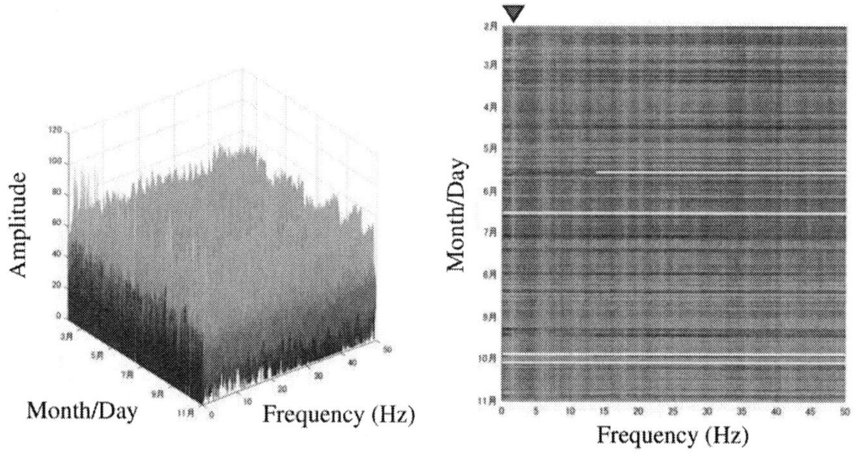

(b) y direction

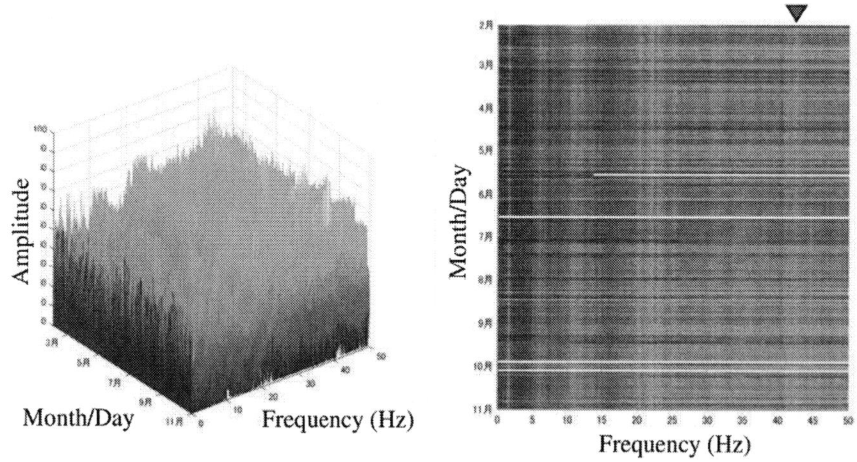

(c) z direction

Figure 3. Fourier spectra of measured data at the top of the tower obtained by accelerometer during the measurement period.

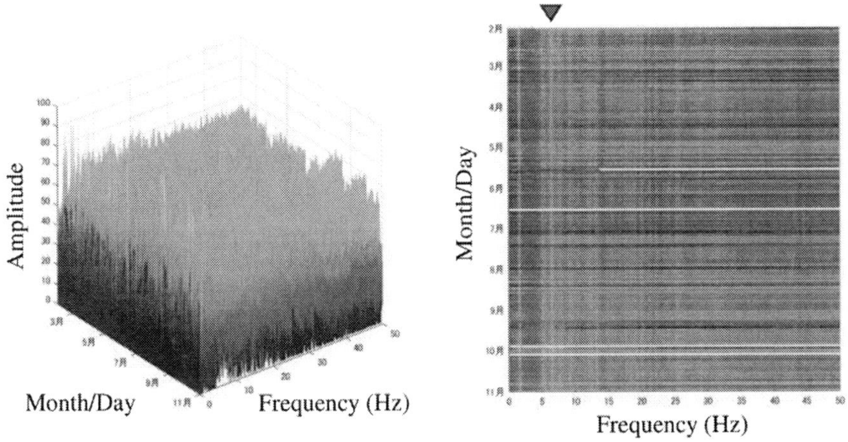

(a) x direction

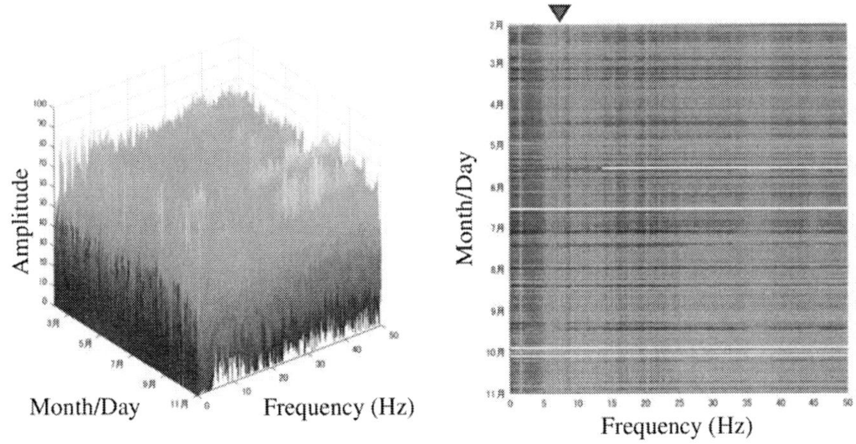

(b) y direction

Figure 4. Fourier spectra of measured data at the top of the tower obtained by accelerometer during the measurement period.

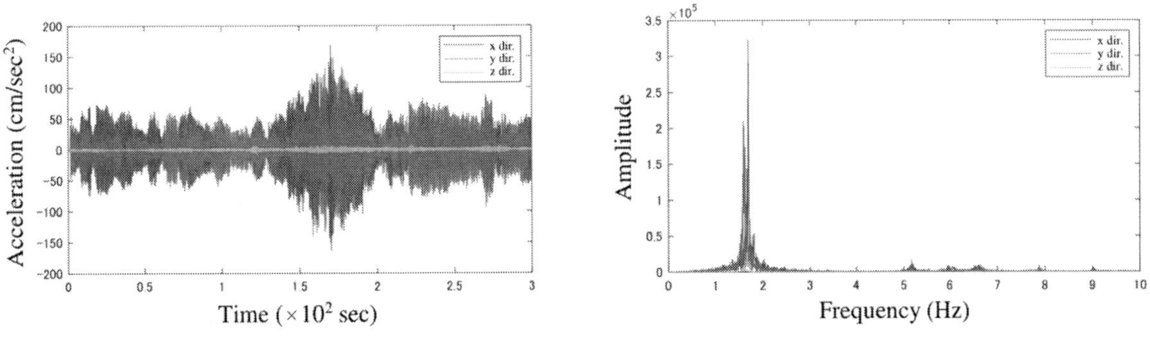

Figure 5. Fourier spectra of measured data at the top of the tower obtained by accelerometer during the measurement period.

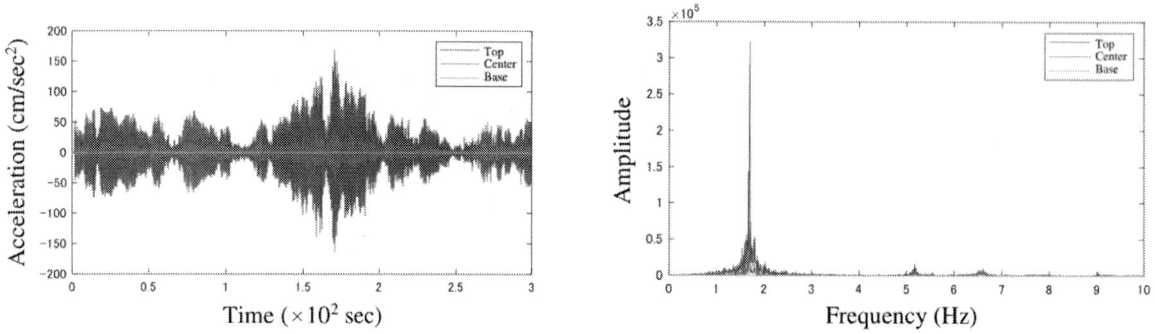

Figure 6. Fourier spectra of measured data at the top of the tower obtained by accelerometer during the measurement period (x direction).

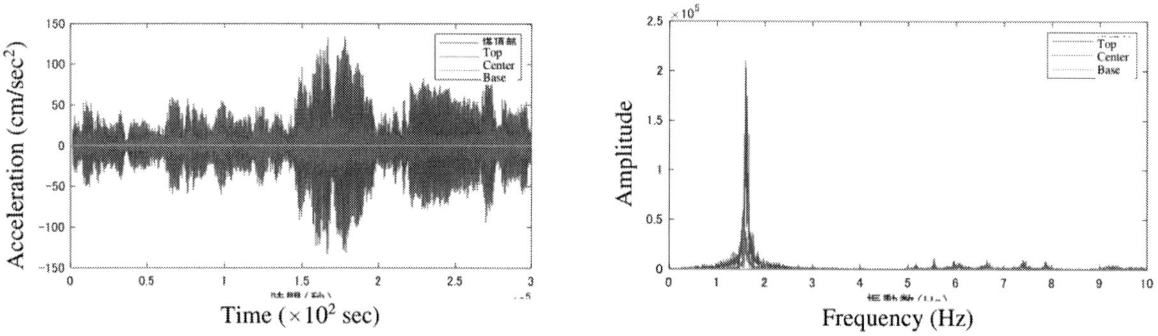

Figure 7. Fourier spectra of measured data at the top of the tower obtained by accelerometer during the measurement period (y direction).

V. CONCLUSION

In the present study, sensors were installed on steel towers, and measurement data was collected and analyzed over a period of several months in order to obtain knowledge useful for monitoring the health of steel tower structures, extending their service life, and equalizing and facilitating reconstruction work. From the measurements and data analysis over a period of nine months, it was found that in the targeted steel tower structures, vibrations at the first-order natural frequencies were dominant, but the higher-order mode natural frequencies were also identified. Continuous monitoring of the natural frequencies of tower structures is considered effective as an indicator of damage risk. If a change in the damage risk indicator occurs, specifically if a trend towards lower natural frequencies is detected, it can be assumed that the rigidity of the structure has decreased, and this can lead to a higher priority for detailed inspection and planned reconstruction work. As a future issue, although the deterioration of the structural performance of the tower over time can be obtained through such fixed-point data measurement and analysis, it would be desirable to acquire data on events during typhoons and other strong winds and earthquakes, when the risk of tower collapse is high, together with video images to understand what events are occurring at that time. and to develop a measurement system to ensure their time synchronization.

ACKNOWLEDGMENT

This research was supported by the Ohata Zaidan, to which the author would like to express gratitude and was partially supported by JSPS KAKENHI Grant Number JP23K04342.

REFERENCES

[1] http://www.mlit.go.jp/road/ir/ir-council/tunnel/pdf/130618_houkoku.pdf, 2013, in Japanese.

[2] https://www.meti.go.jp/shingikai/sankoshin/hoan_shohi/denryoku_anzen/tettou/pdf/001_04_00.pdf, 2019, in Japanese.

[3] https://www.meti.go.jp/shingikai/sankoshin/hoan_shohi/denryoku_anzen/tettou/pdf/20200121_report_01.pdf, 2020, in Japanese.

[4] Y. Liu and S. Nayak, "Structural Health Monitoring: State of the Art and Perspectives," JOM 64, pp. 789–792, 2012, doi: 10.1007/s11837-012-0370-9.

[5] Y. Bao et al., "The State of the Art of Data Science and Engineering in Structural Health Monitorng," Engineering, vol. 5, issue 2, pp. 234-242, 2019, doi: 10.1016/j.eng.2018.11.027.

[6] P. C. Chang, A. Flatau, and S. C. Liu, "Review Paper: Health Monitoring of Civil Infrastructure," Structural Health Monitoring 2003, vol. 2, Issue 3, pp. 257-267, DOI: 10.1177/1475921703036169.

[7] J. P. Lynch, H. Sohn, and M. L. Wang, "Sensor Technologies for Civil Infrastructures," vol. 1: Sensing Hardware and Data Collection Methods for Performance Assessment, ISBN: 978-0-08-102696-0, doi: 10.1016/C2017-0-02662-9.

[8] C. R. Farrar and K. Worden, "Structural Health Monitoring: A Machine Learning Perspective," John Wiley & Sons, Jan. 2013, ISBN: 978-1-119-99433-6, doi:10.1002/9781118443118.

[9] A. R. Al-Ali et al., "An IoT-Based Road Bridge Health Monitoring and Warning System," Sensors 2024, vol. 24, pp. 469-491, doi:10.3390/s24020469.

Gait Analysis of Healthy and Parkinson's Disease Patients in Elderly Population Using FMCW Radar

Sohaib Abdullah[1], Shahzad Ahmed[1], Chanwoo Choi[1], Hee-Jin Kim[2], Kyung Hae Choi[2], and Sung Ho Cho[1,*]
[1]Department of Electronic Engineering, Hanyang University, Seoul, South Korea
[2]Department of Neurology, College of Medicine, Hanyang University, Seoul, South Korea
E-mail: {engrsohaib79[1], shahzad1[1], choi231121[1], dragon[1,*]}@hanyang.ac.kr
hyumcbrain@hanyang.ac.kr[2], choikh73@hanmail.net[2]
*Correspondence: Sung Ho Cho, dragon@hanyang.ac.kr

***Abstract*—Parkinson's Disease (PD) is a prevalent neurological disorder among elderly individuals, resulting in reduced gait control. Technological advancements have brought us many PD sensors based on gait analysis. Amongst these solutions, Radio Frequency (RF) sensors such as, Frequency Modulated Continuous Wave (FMCW) radars have been increasingly used due to their non-invasive nature and ability to operate across different lighting conditions. This study aims to assess the possibility of using FMCW radar-extracted gait parameters for PD detection. Four gait parameters were extracted using radar and reference Inertial Measurement Unit (IMU) sensors from twenty elderly participants including ten control and ten PD patients. The results suggest that FMCW radar can effectively measure step time, step length, step speed, and cadence with Mean Absolute Percentage Error (MAPE) of 8.8%, 10.17%, 9.01%, and 2.82%, respectively. Based on these parameters, gait asymmetry was also measured. The difference between the control group and the PD group in terms of the aforementioned parameters is used to verify the effectiveness of using radar for PD screening.**

Keywords*—*gait analysis, elderly care, Parkinson's disease, FMCW radar.

I. Introduction

The rise in life expectancy of the first world countries [1] has given rise to detective and preventive healthcare research. Particularly, in-home remote health sensing can be a useful early screening tool for several diseases. Remote healthcare sensing empowered by Artificial Intelligence (AI) has enabled several personalized healthcare solutions for the high risk (aging) population [2] [3].

Parkinson's disease (PD) is a frequently occurring neurodegenerative disorder in elderly individuals which is characterized by motor symptoms such as, slowness of movement speed (bradykinesia), rest tremor, and rigidity, and the alterations in spatiotemporal parameters of gait can indicate bradykinesia in PD [4]. Gait analysis can also help distinguish PD patients with non-motor mental symptoms, showing that these patients exhibit a distinct gait pattern characterized by increased slowness and dynamic instability [5]. For this purpose, an extensive amount of research on gait analysis using several different methods has been published. These methods employ Inertial Measurement Units (IMUs), pressure sensitive electronic walkways, optical sensors, and RF sensors, such as radars, for gait analysis.

For gait evaluation using IMU sensors, the devices are typically attached to the lower limbs, such as the feet, shanks, ankles, or knees. An IMU unit includes gyroscope, accelerometer, and magnetometer sensors to collect data on velocity, acceleration, and positional information. Several research works have employed IMU sensors for gait parameters extraction [6]–[9]. For instance, an IMU-based gait study [10] involved attaching IMU sensors to the shanks of both legs of healthy participants, who were then asked to walk a 40-meter distance. Parameters such as stride time, stance time, swing time, step time, step length, stride length, and cadence were calculated.

Despite the high performance of IMU sensors, it can be challenging for patients to walk for long duration while wearing multiple sensors. In contrast, the RF sensors such as radars can measure gait parameters without direct contact with the human subject. For this purpose, a Frequency Modulated Continuous Wave radar is often used. An FMCW radar transmits electromagnetic signals with frequency linearly increasing with time. These radars are extensively used for gesture recognition [11], patient vital sign monitoring [3], activity recognition in long-term care facilities [12], posture estimation [13] and fall detection [14].

Seifert et al. [15] used a continuous wave radar along with a motion capture system to analyze the walking patterns of nineteen participants on a treadmill. Several gait parameters, including stride time, stride length, stance time, flight time, step time, step length, and cadence, were extracted. The errors were found to be negligible, although the study employed two radars. Similarly, walking patterns were also extracted using a doppler radar through trunk velocity and leg velocity. While step characteristics (step time and step length) remained same, the errors for stride-related measurements were higher when extracted using trunk velocity. Another study [16] employed FMCW radar to extract various parameters by mounting the radar on a treadmill and evaluated gait asymmetry. In a more recent study [17], gait asymmetry was evaluated using FMCW radar for both normal and induced abnormal walking. However, it is important to note that these methodologies were not tested on real patients.

In this paper, gait analysis of both healthy individuals and PD patients is performed using an FMCW radar. For all participants, the parameters step time, step length, step velocity, and cadence were extracted and compared with data obtained from IMU sensors. These parameters were collected within a six meters walking (three meters round-trip including

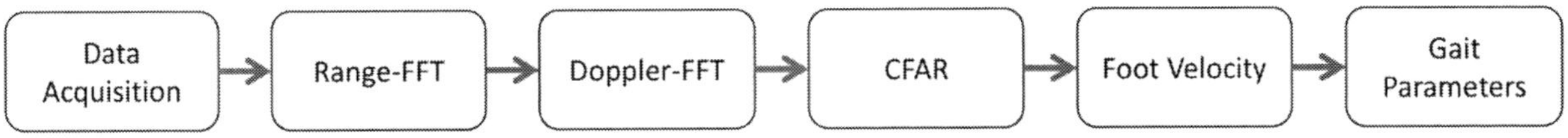

Figure 1. End-to-end block diagram for gait parameters extraction from FMCW radar.

turning point). Additionally, the measured parameters were compared between healthy individuals and PD patients to identify which parameters best describe the walking patterns of PD patients. Gait asymmetry was also evaluated using already established metric, and behavior of participants was analyzed on the turning point using radar. To the best of our knowledge, this study is the first to evaluate gait in real patients and observe the turning behavior using an FMCW radar.

The rest of the paper is organized as follows. Section II explains the proposed methodology, Section III describes the experimental setup, Section IV discusses the results and the conclusions are presented in Section V.

II. Methodology

This section discusses the proposed methodology of radar-based gait analysis in detail. Figure 1 gives an overview of the methodology.

A. Radar Signal Pre-processing

An FMCW radar emits electromagnetic waves with frequency which increases linearly in time, known as chirps. These transmitted signals have a base frequency known as (f_c) and sweep a bandwidth (B) defined by chirp's slope (S) and duration (T_c). The transmitted signal $x(t)$ can be mathematically represented as:

$$x(t) = exp(j2\pi(f_c t + \frac{B}{T_c}t^2)) \quad (1)$$

These chirps collide with a walking human present within the unambiguous range of the radar, and received at receiver antennas after a delay τ_d. To extract the velocity profile of the target human, multiple chirps are transmitted together in a frame. The reflected signals can be represented as:

$$y(t) = exp(j2\pi(f_c(t-\tau) + \frac{B}{T_c}(t-\tau_d)^2)). \quad (2)$$

All the received chirps are mixed with a copy of transmitted chirps to form a single-frequency signals, called Intermediate Frequency (IF) signal. The IF signals for each chirp frame are sampled and stored in a matrix and is further processed to extract different gait parameters.

B. Fast Fourier Transform (FFT) Processing

The two-dimensional matrix contains Analog to Digital Converter (ADC) samples for each IF signal. A Fast Fourier Transform (FFT) is performed on the ADC samples of each transmitted chirp to resolve the range of the target (range-FFT). Another FFT, known as Doppler-FFT is computed on number of chirps in a frame to find the velocity of the target. For range-FFT and Doppler-FFT, FFT sizes of 256 and 128 were used. In this way, a range-Doppler map is created for each frame.

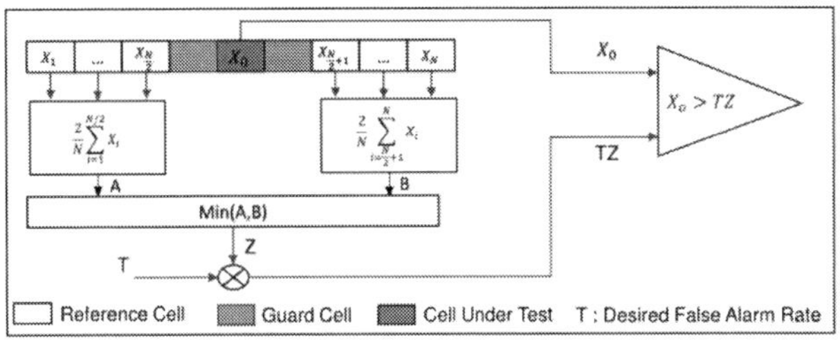

Figure 2. Working principle of CASO-CFAR detection.

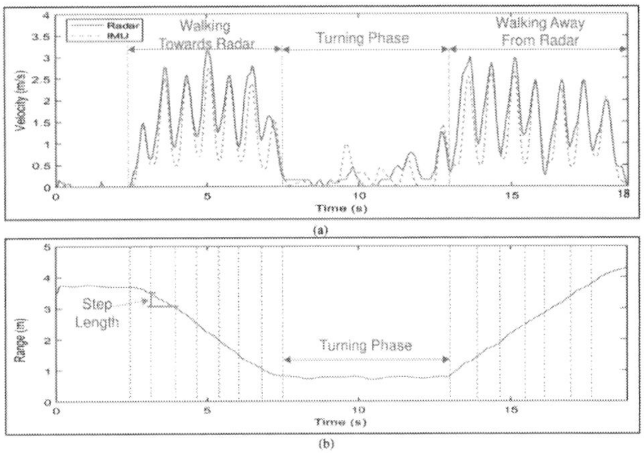

Figure 3. Graphs representing (a) Changes in velocity of the participant measured from radar and IMU during complete walking cycle and (b) Range-time information from radar to measure step length identified through step time marked by consecutive minima in velocity-time graph.

C. Foot Velocity Extraction

After range-FFT and Doppler-FFT processing, the obtained range-Doppler maps contain reflections from human and multipath. So, a 2D Cell-Averaging Smallest of-Constant False Alarm Rate (CASO-CFAR) detection is applied to identify valid target reflections and neglect noise. The CASO-CFAR selects the smallest average from the left and right reference cells as noise level and compares it with signal present in Cell Under Test (CUT) using a desired false alarm rate [18]. The working principle of CASO-CFAR is also shown in Figure 2. In order to enhance the robustness, the CFAR was first applied in range dimension and then in Doppler dimension and only the targets confirmed in the second pass were selected. In our case, the number of reference cells and guard cells both were specified as 8. For a radar positioned at the feet of a human in motion, the foot velocity can be quantified by finding and accumulating the peak with the maximum velocity over time. For IMU sensor, the linear velocity is averaged from x,y and z-axis to obtain reference velocity. Figure 3 (a) show the foot velocity extracted from FMCW radar and IMU sensors.

D. Gait Parameters

In the foot velocity profile, the number of local peaks correspond to the number of steps. In the case of RF-based gait analysis technique, the toe-off and heel-strike cannot be differentiated properly. Hence, an estimate of gait parameters can be provided by identifying two consecutive local minima as toe-off and heel-strike events. Similar strategy was used to derive parameters from IMU sensors. Using this assumption, following spatio-temporal gait parameters can be measured:

1) Step Time: Step time refers to the duration of time taken for one complete step, usually measured in seconds. It is the time interval between the initiation of one foot's contact with the ground and the subsequent contact of the other foot. For the case of radar, step time can be measured by measuring the time difference between two consecutive minima in velocity profile, as expressed below,

$$T_{step}(i) = t_{HS}(i+1) - t_{HS}(i), \tag{3}$$

where $T_{step}(i)$ is the i_{th} step time, $t_{HS}(i)$ and $t_{HS}(i+1)$ are the times at which two consecutive minima in the velocity profile occur.

2) Step Velocity: Step velocity is the speed at which a person walks each step. It can be measured by averaging the instantaneous velocities in a single step.

$$V_{step} = \frac{1}{t}\sum_{n=1}^{t} V(n), \tag{4}$$

where V_{step} is the step velocity, $V(n)$ is instantaneous velocity at instant n, and t represent total number of sampling points within one step.

3) Step Length: Step length is the distance measured from the placement of one foot on the ground to the placement of the opposite foot. For radar, step length can be estimated from range-FFT by utilizing the step time measured previously, as shown in Figure 3 (b), and can be expressed as:

$$L_{step}(i) = r_{HS}(i+1) - r_{HS}(i), \tag{5}$$

where L_{step} is the step length of step i, $r_{HS}(i)$ and $r_{HS}(i+1)$ is the range of human body at two consecutive heel strikes.

TABLE I. DEMOGRAPHIC AND PHYSICAL CHARACTERISTICS OF STUDY PARTICIPANTS.

Parameter	Value
Age (years)	76.89±7.06
Sex (male)	55.5%
Height (m)	1.59±0.08
Weight (kg)	63.33±8.19

4) Cadence: Cadence refers to the number of steps taken per minute. In the case of radar, cadence can be computed by dividing the number of detected steps by total walking time. It is usually expressed as steps per minute (steps/min).

$$Cadence = \frac{\text{Number of Steps}}{\text{Total Walking Time}} \tag{6}$$

III. Experimental Details

This section provide information about the participants, explains the detailed experimental design and configuration of radar and IMU sensors.

A. Participants

Ten patients diagnosed with PD, and ten control volunteered for the study. The additional information such as, age, sex, height and weight is listed in TABLE I in the form of mean±standard deviation. It was made sure that patients did not have any injury of lower limbs that caused any abnormal walking pattern, and that they could walk alone without assistance. All the participants signed a written consent form before taking the experiment.

B. Experimental Setup

The experiments were conducted in the corridor of university hospital. The experimental environment and the details of radar and IMU sensors used are presented in Figure 4(a). The radar was installed at 20cm height. The IMU sensor was also attached to each foot. The participants were asked to walk 3m towards radar, take a 180° turn, and walk 3m again, towards initial starting point, in a continuous manner. The overall experimental setup including positioning of radar and IMUs, walking path and turning point is shown in Figure 4(b).

C. Radar and IMU Configuration

The radar used was Texas Instruments IWR6843ISK and E2box EBIMU24GV5 chipset was used as reference IMU sensor. Both the IMU unit and radar were properly synchronized by matching the starting time and any discrepancies were removed through received timestamps. The operating frequency of radar was 60 GHz and a bandwidth of 3.98 GHz was selected. The slow time sampling rate was 20 FPS and a total of 64 chirps were transmitted in a single frame. All the parameters for radar are listed in TABLE II. Depending on their walking speed, participants completed the walking path in varying duration. Therefore, the radar data capture time was initially set to 25 seconds and the data was later cropped to match the duration of each participant's walking. For IMU, the base frequency was 2.4 GHz and the sampling rate was 100 FPS which was later down-sampled to match with the radar.

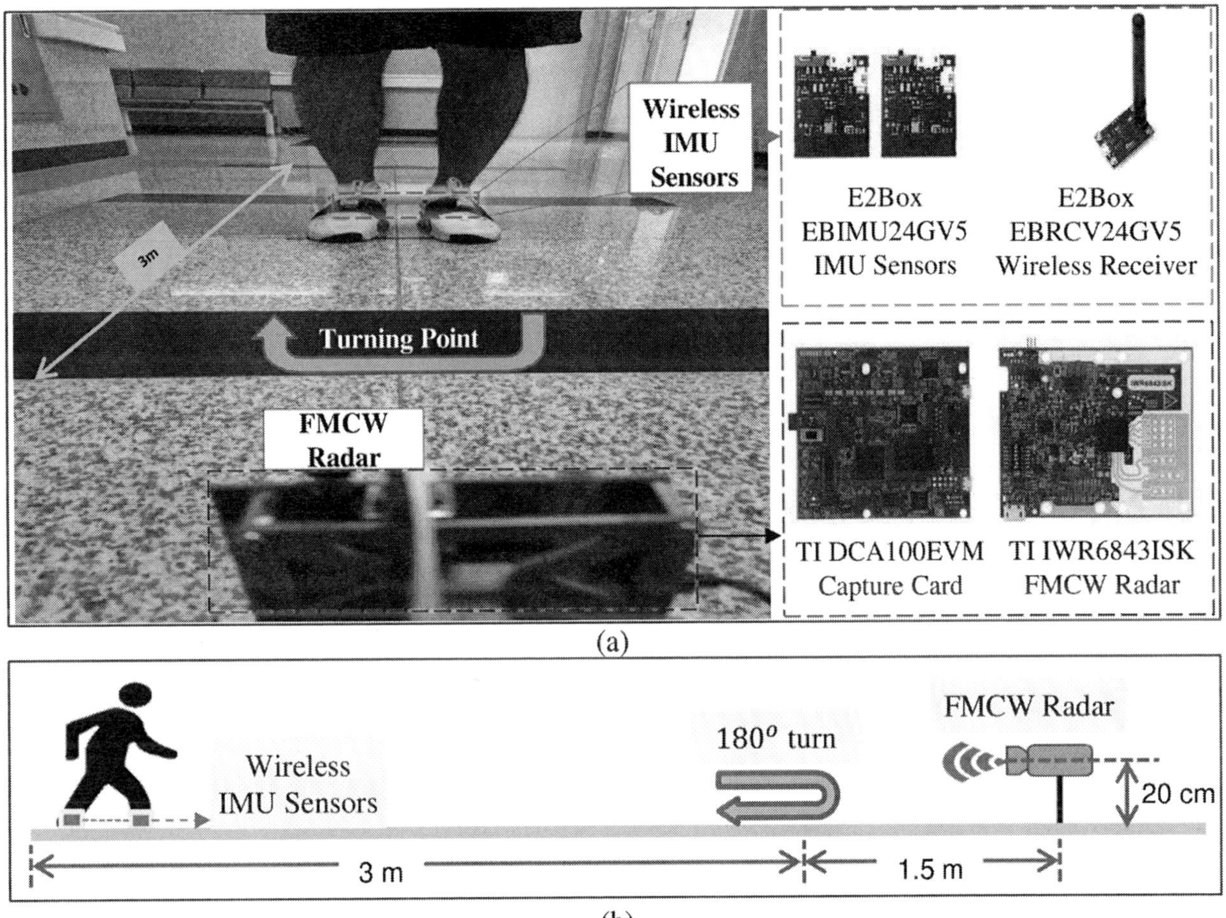

Figure 4. Experimental setup depicting (a) data capturing environment and detail of the employed sensors and (b) radar height, walking path, and turning point.

TABLE II. PARAMETERS USED FOR RADAR CONFIGURATION.

Parameter	Value
Operating Frequency	60 GHz
Sweep bandwidth	3.98 GHz
Number of frames / sec	20
Number of chirps / frame	64
ADC samples / chirp	128
Number of TX antenna	2
Number of RX antenna	4

IV. Results and Discussion

This section presents the obtained results and discusses the findings in detail.

A. Performance Comparison

After the extraction of gait parameters, the values for all the steps were compared with the reference and two error metrics, Mean Absolute Error (MAE) and Mean Absolute Percentage Error (MAPE) were calculated as follows,

$$\mathrm{MAE} = \frac{1}{n}\sum_{t=1}^{n}|A_t - F_t| \tag{7}$$

$$\mathrm{MAPE} = \frac{1}{n}\sum_{t=1}^{n}\left|\frac{A_t - F_t}{A_t}\right| \times 100\% \tag{8}$$

where n is number of detected steps, A_t and F_t is actual (IMU) and predicted (radar) value of the gait parameter for t_{th} step.

TABLE III. RESULTS OBTAINED FOR CONTROL GROUP.

Gait Parameter	Radar Value	IMU Value	MAE	MAPE (%)
Step Time (s)	0.66±0.46	0.67±0.06	0.06	8.32
Step Length (cm)	47.8±6.42	47.3±7.38	4.79	9.91
Step Velocity (m/s)	1.5±0.17	1.41±0.18	0.11	8.45
Cadence $(steps/min)$	38.56±6.19	38.56±6.19	0.80	2.08

The values obtained for step time, step distance, step velocity and cadence along with the errors are presented in TABLES III and IV, for control and patient group, respectively. By looking at the MAE, it can be seen that the control group showed slightly higher error rate in terms of step length and slightly lower error for the case of cadence, whereas similar

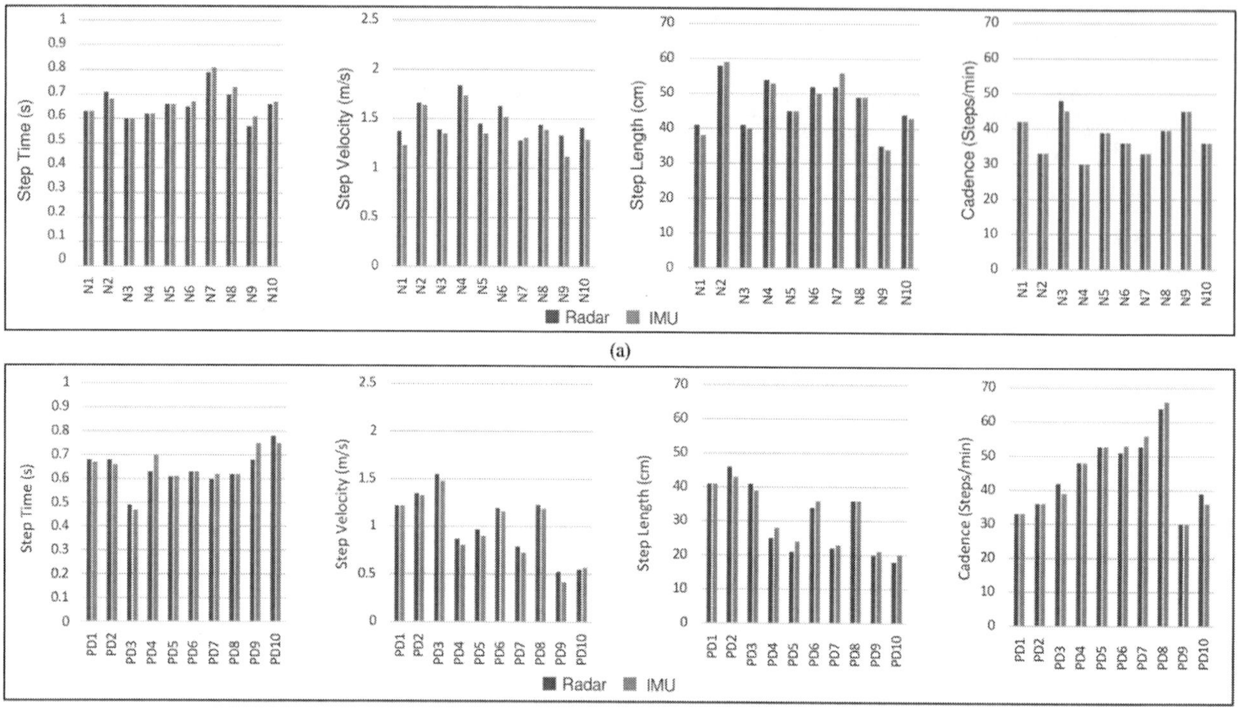

(a)

(b)

Figure 5. Graphs showing agreement of gait parameters (step time, step length, step velocity and cadence) extracted from radar and IMU for (a) control group and (b) patient group.

error rates were observed for step time and step velocity. However, the MAPE shows consistently higher error rates for PD patients for all the parameters, due to the fact that it depends heavily on the scale of the actual values. As the PD patients show smaller values of gait parameters than control group (except cadence), consequently, their percentage error appeared as higher, even for same MAE (as for the case of step velocity). Figure 5 shows mean values of all the gait parameters obtained from radar and IMU sensors for all the participants.

B. Unique Patterns between Control and Patient Group

Once the parameters were extracted, the values were compared among both groups using Mann-Whitney U-test and the p-values are listed in TABLE V. It was found that the control group exhibited significantly greater step length ($p<0.01$) and step velocity ($p<0.01$) while no considerable difference was found in terms of step time ($p>0.05$) and cadence ($p>0.05$). The patients suffering from PD can have limited range of motion of lower limbs, thereby reducing step (or stride) lengths and overall walking speed [19]. Additionally, for MAPE, no statistically significant difference was found in the control and the PD group. The average values for each each gait parameter for both groups are also shown in Figure 6.

TABLE IV. RESULTS OBTAINED FOR PATIENT GROUP.

Gait Parameter	Radar Value	IMU Value	MAE	MAPE (%)
Step Time (s)	0.63±0.05	0.64±0.05	0.06	9.43
Step Length (cm)	34.2±11.77	34±9.88	3.5	10.43
Step Velocity (m/s)	1.14±0.42	1.09±0.41	0.11	9.58
Cadence $(steps/min)$	48.76±12.1	48.39±12.22	1.72	3.56

TABLE V. COMPARISON OF RADAR-BASED GAIT PARAMETERS AMONG CONTROL AND PATIENT GROUP. THE PARAMETERS WITH AN ASTERISK(*) WERE FOUND TO BE STATISTICALLY SIGNIFICANT.

Parameter	Control Group	Patient Group	*p-value*
Step Time (s)	0.66±0.46	0.63±0.05	0.622
Step Length (cm)*	47.8±6.42	34.2±11.77	0.003
Step Velocity (m/s)*	1.5±0.17	1.14±0.42	0.002
Cadence (steps/min)	38.56±6.19	48.76±12.1	0.16
MAPE for Step Time (%)	8.32±2.61	9.43±3.98	0.97
MAPE for Step Length (%)	9.91±1.56	10.43±1.91	0.113
MAPE for Step Velocity (%)	8.45±1.76	9.58±2.21	0.678
MAPE for Cadence (%)	2.08±1.84	3.56±3.28	0.99

C. Gait Asymmetry

The steps of all the participants were separated and the asymmetry between even and odd numbered steps was calculated using two different metrics, Symmetry Index (SI) [20]

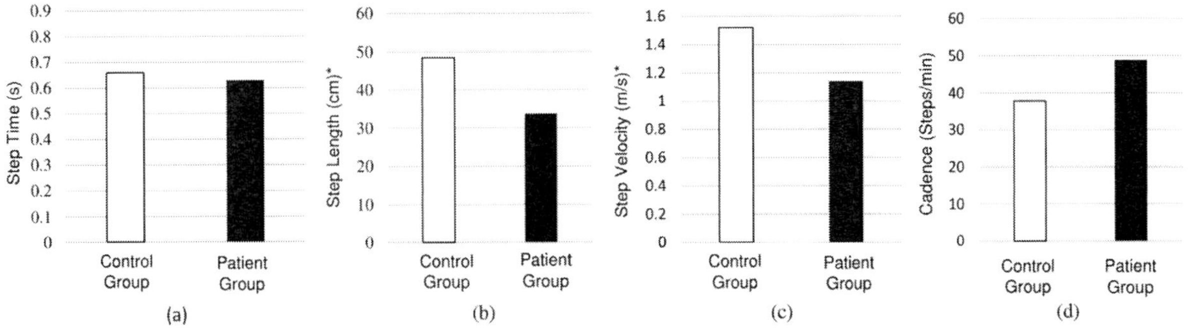

Figure 6. Comparison of gait parameters (a) step time, (b) step length, (c) step velocity, and (d) cadence, obtained from radar for the control and patient groups. Patient group exhibited smaller step length with lower step velocity and higher cadence than control group. The parameter with an asterisk(*) were found to be statistically significant ($p<0.01$).

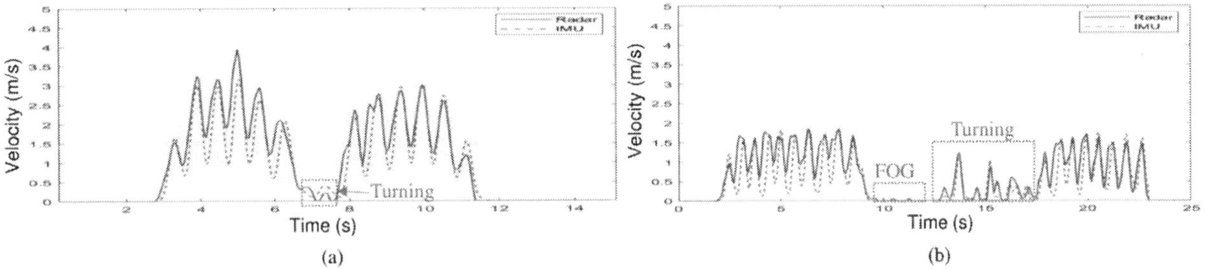

Figure 7. Velocity profiles of (a) healthy participant who took one single step quickly to complete the turn and (b) PD patient who suffered from Freezing of Gait (FOG) and took multiple steps.

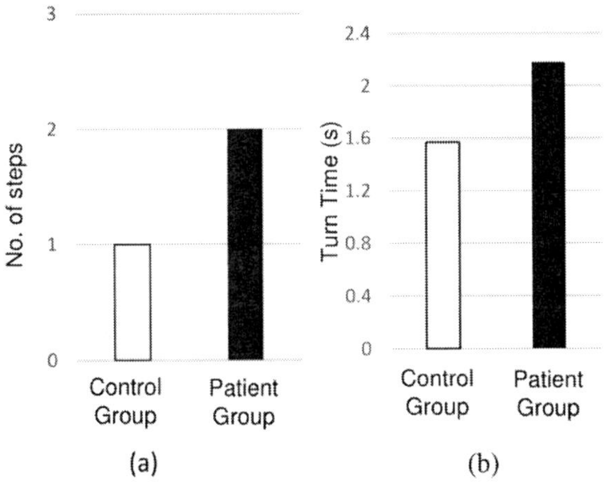

Figure 8. Comparison of (a) number of steps and (b) amount of time taken while turning. Patient group took more steps and time to complete the turn.

and Gait Asymmetry (GA) [21],

$$GA = |ln\{\frac{min(X_{even}, X_{odd})}{max(X_{even}, X_{odd})}\}| \times 100\% \quad (9)$$

$$SI = \frac{|X_{even} - X_{odd}|}{0.5(X_{even} + X_{odd})} \times 100\% \quad (10)$$

where X_{even} and X_{odd} refer to the average value of the gait parameter under consideration, for even and odd numbered step, respectively. A value of 0% indicate complete symmetry while 100% means complete asymmetry.

TABLE VI. MEASURE OF GAIT ASYMMETRY FOR CONTROL AND PATIENT GROUP.

Gait Parameter	Control Group	Patient Group	*p-value*
Step Time GA(%)	9.87±6.01	7.64±5.07	0.39
Step Length GA(%)	9.57±7.16	24.45±12.57	0.02
Step Velocity GA(%)	3.15±2.58	8.21±9.81	0.04

Using (9) and (10), the gait asymmetry and symmetry index was calculated for step time, step speed and step length. The use of the above two relations resulted in similar values. Subsequently, the statistical significance was also assessed between the control and PD groups using previously mentioned statistical test. The measure of gait asymmetry for both groups along with the p-values are presented in TABLE VI. It was found that patient group had higher step length asymmetry ($p<0.05$) and step velocity asymmetry ($p<0.05$) while no significant differences were found in step time asymmetry ($p>0.05$). The step length asymmetry in PD patients can be linked to reduced structural connectivity in the sensorimotor corpus callosum, compared to the control group [22].

D. Turning in Control and Patients Group

Mostly, research on gait analysis in individuals with PD emphasizes straight-line walking, however, turning difficulties are an early indicator of PD progression as individuals with PD require more time and steps to complete a turn [23]. Hence, analysis of turning behavior can provide meaningful insight into the health of PD patients. For radar, the starting of the turning phase can be marked through a sharp reduction in velocity while the end of turning can be recognized through multiple consecutive high velocity peaks in the velocity-time plot. In this way, the turning phase was analyzed for healthy and patient's data. Figure 7 shows an example of turning phase identification for one healthy subject and one patient.

After identifying the turning phases, the number of steps and time was measured for both groups and a graph was plotted. Figure 8 (a) shows the number of steps and Figure 8 (b) shows the time taken while turning for both control group and patient group. It can be seen that the patient group took more steps and longer time to turn. The turning ability in PD can be hindered by limited trunk flexibility, problems with turn coordination, freezing episodes, and balance issues [24], therefore, they complete the turn in multiple steps in order to avoid fall [23].

V. Conclusion

This study demonstrates the potential of FMCW radar in measuring gait parameters for individuals with PD and healthy controls. The analysis focused on four key gait parameters namely step time, step length, step speed, and cadence. On comparing the performance of radar data with IMU sensor, the results show a MAPE of 8.8% for step time, 10.17% for step length, 9.01% for step speed, and 2.82% for cadence.

Additionally, the study highlights the radar's ability to detect gait asymmetry and analyze walking patterns at the turning point. These findings suggest that the FMCW radar can serve as a viable, non-invasive tool for gait monitoring in daily living scenarios, potentially aiding in early intervention and better management of PD.

Acknowledgment

This study was supported by the National Research Foundation (NRF) of South Korea (NRF-2022R1A2C2008783). This study received approval for all ethical and experimental procedures from the Institutional Review Board on Human Subjects Research and Ethics Committees at Hanyang University in Seoul, South Korea, under Approval No. HYUH 2023-10-035-004.

References

[1] L. F. Berkman and B. C. Truesdale, "Working longer and population aging in the us: Why delayed retirement isn'ta practical solution for many," *The Journal of the Economics of Ageing*, vol. 24, p. 100438, 2023.

[2] M. Arsalan, M. Owais, T. Mahmood, J. Choi, and K. R. Park, "Artificial intelligence-based diagnosis of cardiac and related diseases," *Journal of Clinical Medicine*, vol. 9, no. 3, p. 871, 2020.

[3] S. Ahmed and S. H. Cho, "Machine learning for healthcare radars: Recent progresses in human vital sign measurement and activity recognition," *IEEE Communications Surveys & Tutorials*, vol. 26, no. 1, pp. 461–495, 2023.

[4] L. Ma *et al.*, "Gait variability is sensitive to detect parkinson's disease patients at high fall risk," *International Journal of Neuroscience*, vol. 132, no. 9, pp. 888–893, 2022.

[5] M. Russo *et al.*, "Interplay between gait and neuropsychiatric symptoms in parkinson's disease," *European Journal of Translational Myology*, vol. 32, no. 2, 2022.

[6] N. Muthukrishnan, J. J. Abbas, and N. Krishnamurthi, "A wearable sensor system to measure step-based gait parameters for parkinson's disease rehabilitation," *Sensors*, vol. 20, no. 22, p. 6417, 2020.

[7] M. Zago *et al.*, "Gait evaluation using inertial measurement units in subjects with parkinson's disease," *Journal of Electromyography and Kinesiology*, vol. 42, pp. 44–48, 2018.

[8] H. Zhao, Z. Wang, S. Qiu, Y. Shen, and J. Wang, "Imu-based gait analysis for rehabilitation assessment of patients with gait disorders," in *2017 4th International Conference on Systems and Informatics (ICSAI)*. IEEE, 2017, pp. 622–626.

[9] L. Zhou *et al.*, "Validation of an imu gait analysis algorithm for gait monitoring in daily life situations," in *2020 42nd Annual International Conference of the IEEE Engineering in Medicine & Biology Society (EMBC)*. IEEE, 2020, pp. 4229–4232.

[10] T. Gujarathi and K. Bhole, "Gait analysis using imu sensor," in *2019 10th International Conference on Computing, Communication and Networking Technologies (ICCCNT)*. IEEE, 2019, pp. 1–5.

[11] S. Ahmed and S. H. Cho, "Hand gesture recognition using an ir-uwb radar with an inception module-based classifier," *Sensors*, vol. 20, no. 2, p. 564, 2020.

[12] H. Abedi *et al.*, "Ai-powered non-contact in-home gait monitoring and activity recognition system based on mm-wave fmcw radar and cloud computing," *IEEE Internet of Things Journal*, vol. 10, no. 11, pp. 9465 – 9481, 2023.

[13] J. Lee, K. Park, and Y. Kim, "Deep learning-based device-free localization scheme for simultaneous estimation of indoor location and posture using fmcw radars," *Sensors*, vol. 22, no. 12, p. 4447, 2022.

[14] Y. Yao *et al.*, "Unsupervised learning-based unobtrusive fall detection using fmcw radar," *IEEE Internet of Things Journal*, vol. 11, no. 3, pp. 5078–5089, 2023.

[15] A.-K. Seifert, M. Grimmer, and A. M. Zoubir, "Doppler radar for the extraction of biomechanical parameters in gait analysis," *IEEE Journal of Biomedical and Health Informatics*, vol. 25, no. 2, pp. 547–558, 2020.

[16] D. Wang, J. Park, H.-J. Kim, K. Lee, and S. H. Cho, "Noncontact extraction of biomechanical parameters in gait analysis using a multi-input and multi-output radar sensor," *IEEE Access*, vol. 9, pp. 138 496–138 508, 2021.

[17] S. Ahmed, Y. Seo, and S. H. Cho, "Gait asymmetry evaluation using fmcw radar in daily life environments," in *International Work-Conference on Bioinformatics and Biomedical Engineering*. Springer, 2023, pp. 116–127.

[18] J. Zhu, X. Huang, J. Liu, and Z. Deng, "Robust cfar detector based on clean for sidelobe suppression," *IEEE Sensors Journal*, vol. 24, no. 9, pp. 14 930 – 14 942, 2024.

[19] A. P. J. Zanardi *et al.*, "Gait parameters of parkinson's disease compared with healthy controls: A systematic review and meta-analysis," *Scientific reports*, vol. 11, no. 1, p. 752, 2021.

[20] K. K. Patterson, W. H. Gage, D. Brooks, S. E. Black, and W. E. McIlroy, "Evaluation of gait symmetry after stroke: a comparison of current methods and recommendations for standardization," *Gait & posture*, vol. 31, no. 2, pp. 241–246, 2010.

[21] A. Sant'Anna, A. Salarian, and N. Wickstrom, "A new measure of movement symmetry in early parkinson's disease patients using symbolic processing of inertial sensor data," *IEEE Transactions on biomedical engineering*, vol. 58, no. 7, pp. 2127–2135, 2011.

[22] B. Fling, C. Curtze, and F. Horak, "Gait asymmetry in people with parkinson's disease is linked to reduced integrity of callosal sensorimotor regions. front neurol 9 (april): 215," 2018.

[23] J. Spildooren, C. Vinken, L. Van Baekel, and A. Nieuwboer, "Turning problems and freezing of gait in parkinson's disease: a systematic review and meta-analysis," *Disability and rehabilitation*, vol. 41, no. 25, pp. 2994–3004, 2019.

[24] A.-M. Willems *et al.*, "Turning in parkinson's disease patients and controls: the effect of auditory cues," *Movement disorders*, vol. 22, no. 13, pp. 1871–1878, 2007.